BARNEY

THE STRAY
BEAGLE
WHO BECAME
A TV STAR
AND STOLE
OUR HEARTS

DICK WOLFSIE

emmis

books

Emmis Books
1700 Madison, 2nd Floor
Cincinnati, Ohio 45206

ISBN 1-57860-167-3

LCCN 2004106140

Photographs of Barney on TV, courtesy of WISH-TV, Channel 8 (Indianapolis)

Designed by Patricia Prather, Dean Johnson Design
Edited by Jessica Yerega and Jack Heffron

DEDICATION

This book is dedicated to pet lovers everywhere, but especially
to Liz Severino, with whom I share a secret about Barney.
I know it is safe with her.

Every dog touches the lives of a few
A few dogs touch the lives of many
In memory of Barney the Beagle

(ON A PLAQUE AT AN INDIANA ANIMAL SHELTER)

To rich
"Best Fishes"

TABLE OF CONTENTS

PREFACE

NO WRITING ASSIGNMENT was ever more fun and so difficult at the same time. More than a few tears have seeped between the letters of my keyboard as I put together Barney's story. Don't feel sorry for me. I also spent a lot of time watching old video footage of my pal with a huge grin on my face.

As you read, you may notice more than one reference to the same anecdote or story. This book is a collection of recollections, previous writings and new observations—not a strictly chronological account of Barney's life. Over the years, I have written, then rewritten, some of my favorite memories. Sometimes the stories get even better. That's the fun of being a writer.

This is not just a celebration of Barney; it is a tribute to all pets who have made our lives happier and more fulfilling. Barney just happened to find my doorstep. Had he found your doorstep, Barney would have meant just as much to you. And you, too, would have had bountiful stories to tell.

Fate brought him to me. And that led to his TV career. Was Barney destined for show business?

Read this book and you'll have little doubt.

INTRODUCTION

BY DR. ALAN BECK, PURDUE UNIVERSITY SCHOOL OF VETERINARY MEDICINE

AS A PERSON who studies the unique connection between humans and their pets, I took a special interest in the duo of Dick Wolfsie and Barney.

Dogs play the role of a family member—often the member with the most desired attributes. For some, dogs afford increased opportunities to meet people, while for others they permit people to be alone without being lonely. Dogs can contribute to a child's development by being the child's child, thus teaching and encouraging a nurturing attitude that will last a lifetime. Dogs can have many therapeutic uses that are only now are being recognized.

Of course, humans are important to dogs, also. Dogs were created by, and are sustained by, people. Dogs thrive by living in groups, or packs, which include humans. Indeed, dogs comprehend human actions more than wolves or even primates. Understanding people appears to be part of their domestication process.

And dogs often steal the spotlight. Lassie, Rin Tin Tin, and Benji are as famous, or perhaps more so, than their human partners. Dick Wolfsie is a delightfully funny TV reporter and author whose warmth was immediately recognized, and perhaps enhanced, by his celebrity canine partner, Barney.

People grew to love both. Actually, I suspect Barney may have had even more fans for he carries none of the potential "baggage" that all people do just because they are human.

Barney looked, or smelled, at each situation with the innocence and objectivity that only a dog can bring. Joining Dick on the morning news interviews, he found each TV segment's subjects interesting; and we all found the show more fun to watch, anticipating his moves.

When Barney died, the response from the public was overwhelming. People felt as though they had lost their own dog. And in a way, they had. For more than twelve years, Barney had been in their living room or kitchen every morning. And he never had an accident. That's a record to be proud of.

Enjoy this book and pretend Barney is with you, as he was with all of us.

DAY ONE

I REMEMBER THE day I met Barney. Wait a second. No, I don't. I haven't a clue what day it was. It was 1991. I know that. And it was cold. Real cold.

It was my first month or so at Channel 8. My new gig involved getting up at 3:30 a.m., stepping on my eyeglasses, stumbling into the shower, putting on two different color socks, and spilling coffee in my lap in the car.

This had become pretty much a routine. Anything that caused me to veer from this schedule threw me off for the rest of the day.

Then on the morning of January 7, or January 21…or was it February 3? I opened my front door and there he was:

AROOOOOOOOOOOOOOOOOOOOOOOOOOOOOOOOOOOOO!
AROOOOOOOOOOOOOOOOOOOOOOOOOOOOOOOOOOOOO!

A tiny beagle. He was acting hungry. Little did I know, he would act hungry for the next fourteen years.

The reason I don't remember the date is that I did not realize then that my life was about to change. This little beagle who had wandered onto my doorstep would not only brighten my life for the next decade and beyond, but he would become Central Indiana's favorite dog.

I wish I had realized that. I would have written down the date. I'm a reporter, you know.

So, now what? My heart went out to the little guy. But I was late for work. I still had an entire cup of coffee to spill on myself. I opened the front door wider and in he walked, like he owned the place. I closed the door and went to work.

You're right. I am an idiot.

Four hours later, I returned to the house. There was no house left. Here's an abbreviated list of what he destroyed:

1. The couch
2. My wife's high heel shoes
3. The curtains
4. The living room rug

As I walked in the door, my five-year-old son, Brett, was descending the stairs with a beheaded teddy bear and an unstuffed lion. Tears rolled down his cheeks. He stared at Barney, then shot a glance at his decapitated playthings.

"Daddy, can we NOT keep him?"

That pretty much said it all. Barney had not made a good first impression. My wife ordered me to return him, a request hard to fulfill because I did not know where he came from.

I do not remember how long Barney remained at home while I went to work. My wife says it seemed about a year or so. It was probably about three days. Then I got the ultimatum from Mary Ellen: "Look, this is real simple: the dog must go. Either that, or take him to work with you."

So there you have it. This brilliant concept of turning a street mutt into a TV celebrity was borne out of my wife's sheer frustration with what was ten pounds of pure trouble. Barney matured, of course, and would later become fifteen, twenty, twenty-five, thirty, thirty-five, and forty pounds of trouble.

And that is what the rest of the book is about.

THE FIRST WEEK

THE FIRST WEEK I took Barney to work was not intended to create a canine superstar; it was to avoid a divorce. Barney had the potential to cause a broken home. And he had done quite a bit to cause a broken house as well.

The first couple of days, I kept Barney in the car while I hosted three early morning segments on "Daybreak," the Channel 8 news show. He wasn't happy. Barney's howl, more like a siren, was so loud that even if my car was a hundred yards away from the TV truck, the bellowing could be heard on TV.

I tried parking the car closer to my reporting location so Barney would not feel abandoned, but this had the opposite effect and even made him more determined to get my attention. The wailing only increased. Because it was winter, most of the segments were indoors. But I was reluctant to request of my guests that Barney be allowed to come into their home or office. I knew what had happened to my own home and office.

One morning when I sensed his bellowing would wake up the neighborhood, I asked permission to bring him into the senior citizens' home in Mooresville, Indiana. The residents were putting on a little talent show and had no problem with Barney being tied up inside. They did stress the words "TIED UP."

The show began and one of the first guests was a very spry octogenarian whose talent was doing the hula. She came out from behind the curtain and began doing the native dance. Her grass skirt was seductively flapping about. Not seductive to me, I assure you, but seductive to a year-old beagle that chased and

STEVE RICHARDSON

3

chewed anything that moved.

Barney, securely tied to a chair (I thought), beagle-eyed the hula dancer's skirt, busted off his lead, and bee-lined to his intended target. In a flash, he grabbed a hunk of the skirt in his teeth and ripped it off the woman. Completely off.

Fortunately, the woman had sufficient undergarments to keep the show rated PG-13, but my cameraman almost broke his neck trying to whip the camera around in order to feature a more family-friendly picture. He was also laughing so hard, we barely got through the rest of the show.

The residents took it pretty well considering they hadn't seen anything quite like that at the Mooresville Senior Citizens' Home for some years.

When we left, we were invited back. By all the men.

For ten years, this was my license plate (with different years, of course). With this plate, I never got a ticket. But I was stopped a few times. I think the police just wanted to meet Barney.

BARNEY'S MANY ADVENTURES

THE ONLY THING that Beagles love as much as food is an open door. When left to roam inside a building, Barney could, despite his girth, manage to squeeze his way through any aperture. If he couldn't find an open door, Barney would find an unsuspecting accomplice, roll his big brown eyes and convince someone that he needed to go outside. Forever.

Then, he was off. Usually I found him at a dumpster, but once he was at the drive-up window of a Hardee's waiting with a bunch of people for the restaurant to open.

Once, in Greenwood, Barney escaped from the show location, a laser tag facility. Based on past experience, he could travel half a mile in about six minutes. He had been gone over an hour.

I ran up and down Meridian Street, bellowing his name. This technique hadn't worked once in the six years since I first found him. He never came when I called him. NEVER. This is a typical beagle trait. I have a book called *The Idiot's Guide to Beagles*, which kinda says it all. The book suggests that if you want your beagle to come when you call, always carry a box of biscuits you can shake.

Hey, that's convenient.

Panicked, I called the local police chief and begged him to put out an APB. I wasn't sure what an APB was, but I knew the police took it seriously. Maybe they would find him.

An hour later, still no Barney. Convinced the dog had disappeared or had been struck by a car, I was about to head home. Suddenly, police sirens and bubble machine lights. The police car rounded the corner at about seventy mph and skidded to a halt next to me in the parking lot.

I looked in. Sitting next to the officer was Barney. Both his front feet and back were in handcuffs.

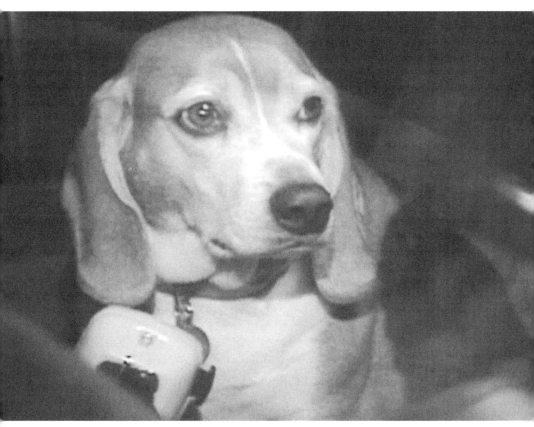

Barney in the police car.

"What happened, Officer?"

"Your dog has been arrested."

"For what?"

"I was off duty and went to Marsh to get some milk for my family. I look up and there's your dog walking down Aisle 4 with a barbecue chicken in his mouth. He's in serious trouble, Mr. Wolfsie. Hoosiers don't take chicken-stealing lightly."

I don't think Barney was officially charged with theft. The people at Marsh are very nice and no charges were pressed.

Barney would have hated prison food.

PUTTING IN MY TWO SCENTS

A TV SEGMENT about how coonhounds can track a raccoon scent seemed like a no-brainer. It was an all-noser. No intelligence involved. The dogs put down their nostrils and they're off.

But what a cool idea for a TV show. Watching dogs sniff. Smell-a-vision.

I met my guests at a southside park where we dragged a raccoon scent along the ground, leading to a tree. "The dogs will follow the scent, wherever it leads," bragged the owners. "They are very smart."

They are? It wasn't even a raccoon. It was just the scent. And you can't eat the scent. You just bark at it. I wasn't going to argue. Guys with coonhounds also carry guns.

"I bet Barney can do this, also," I thought. Barney could smell an unopened package of barbecue potato chips in my glove compartment.

Probably the most replayed segment on Channel 8—and still a howl.

Here was the plan. I brought this huge summer sausage with me to the park and dragged it along the ground, just adjacent to the raccoon scent, but about fifty yards out, the two scents parted (okay, now you understand the title?). The raccoon smell led to the tree and the salami odor led to a picnic area where the summer sausage was placed on top of a table.

Lights, camera, action! Live TV. The dogs were off. The four coonhounds rumbled ahead while Barney, who was beginning to fashion a few extra pounds, managed to waddle up a sweat from behind.

The coonhounds realized that the raccoon scent was trailing to the right. They raced off in hot pursuit. Not Barney. Moments later, viewers saw the little chow hound hop on the picnic table and devour the entire sausage.

The coonhounds were then seen barking up a tree. At nothing.

Who's the smart one now?

Barney decided not to follow his instincts here. He decided to follow the pepperoni.

BARNEY'S FRIENDS

Barney made friends wherever he went . . . and he went every-where.

DAREDEVIL BARNEY

At the Natatorium in 1993, Barney found his way to the top of the highest board. No, he didn't jump.

NOBLE DOG!

I WAS EXCESSIVELY cautious about Barney. When he was outside, I'd check on him every ten minutes to make sure he had not slipped through the Invisible Fence. I once figured out that about 40 percent of my income was directly attributable to him. (No wonder I was paranoid.)

Being over-protective, I likely called the vet more often than most dog and cat owners, too. Here are a couple of times I probably needn't have.

My wife was on a business trip and in order to provide my son with all the basic food groups I ordered an extra-large pizza from Noble Roman's. It was late on a Friday night and Brett and I were about to sit down to dinner when the phone rang.

"It's probably Mom," I said. "I'm going upstairs to take the call. Watch the pizza."

It would be about ten minutes before I first realized what part of "I'm going upstairs to take the call. Watch the pizza," Brett paid no attention to.

When I returned to the kitchen, there was no pizza left. And no box. And I knew that Brett seldom ate the box, so it must have been the canine trash compactor.

The culprit was hiding behind the couch, which was apparently tough for him because before he ate the pizza he weighed forty pounds and now he was tipping the scales at forty-five pounds. He was stuck, wedged between the sofa and table.

I panicked. Barney's tummy was so distended that it scraped along the ground like a Bassett hound's ears. I figured I had to get all that stuff out of his stomach. I knew there was a way. But I had forgotten how. I ran to the phone and called my vet, Bob McCune, who answered the phone from a dead sleep.

"Doc, it's Dick Wolfsie."

"What's the matter?"

"Barney just ate an extra-large pepperoni pizza. What should I give him?"

"A Budweiser?"

Clearly this was not the emergency I thought it was. But it was not the last time I would over-react.

A few weeks later, I heard some noise downstairs in the kitchen. Barney had sometimes made his way down the steps in the middle of the night to see if he could rustle up a snack, so I figured he was pawing at the pantry door where his treats were kept.

I walked down to the kitchen and there was Barney chewing on what appeared to be a piece of aluminum foil. No, it was an ant trap that the beagle had negotiated from beneath the fridge with his paw! The blue "poison" was dripping from his mouth.

I panicked.

I threw him in the car and raced to a local all-night pet emergency clinic. It was 3 a.m. and I began ringing the bell, then banging on the door. A woman veterinarian, who had been sleeping prior to my interruption, came to the entrance. Unfortunately, she recognized me.

"What is it, Mr. Wolfsie? Is Barney okay?"

"He ate an ant trap. Is he going to die?"

"Heavens no," said the vet, "those things don't even kill ants."

That would be the last time I would worry about things he ate.

Author's note: Some ant traps are dangerous to pets, which the vet explained. But after her funny remark she checked the trap (which I had brought with me) and confirmed from the ingredients that Barney would be okay.

A DIRTY STORY

WHAT YOU ARE about to read has probably become the classic Barney story. It happened just months after I first found him on my doorstep back in 1991.

And the whole thing was on live TV. If you don't believe me, I'll show you the tape.

Barney was an inveterate digger. In the first few months I had him, he dug under our wood fence three

Another classic. Dr. Sampson explains why hounds like to dig. And Barney does a live demonstration.

times, dug up the carpet in the living room and dug a hole the size of a Buick in the front yard. He buried a loaf of Italian bread under the covers at the foot of my son's bed. YUK.

At obedience school, I was told that digging is in a beagle's nature. And, as you know if you've had a beer at the RCA Dome, when nature calls it's hard to turn a deaf ear. Imagine if you had beagle ears.

Dr. Gary Sampson is an animal behavior specialist who had heard my complaints about the burying beagle on "Daybreak," WISH-TV's morning news show. "I can help Barney with that," he told me.

"Geez, Doc, the last thing Barney needs is help with it. I want someone to stop him."

Dr. Sampson agreed to come on the show one morning and discuss the issue. Bright and early, Dr. Sampson and I sat on my front porch while he pontificated about the animal instinct to dig and some of the possible remedies.

Barney was unimpressed.

Never in television has a dog taken a cue better than Barney. At the first mention of digging, Barney was on a mission. His first target was my wife's rose bush near the front stoop. The barrage of dirt was so great that both the doc and I spent most of the interview brushing off the remains of his tirade.

Looking at the pile of dirt that had accumulated at his feet and peering at the hound as he continued to excavate, the doctor observed: "There must be something down there that he wants."

That's why these guys make the big bucks.

All this was during the first two segments. During the break, I mentioned to the good doctor that we should probably move from the digging problem to Barney's chewing problem. Dr. Sampson agreed that was a good idea.

We never did do that segment. During the break, Barney chewed the audio cord from the camera. And we never got on the air again.

When Barney died, Gary Sampson wrote me the nicest letter. He said he had very fond memories of Barney. "He will be hard to forget," said the doctor.

Yes, he will, Dr. Sampson. Yes, he will.

BARNEY'S FRIENDS

LIFE IN THE UNDERGROUND

AS YOU MAY have read in another chapter, when Barney was matched up against a pack of professional coonhounds, he performed quite well, although his ultimate goal differed from his competitors': they sought a raccoon; Barney sniffed down a stick of pepperoni.

Still another example of Barney's tremendous breadth of talent was his search and rescue debut. Once again on live TV.

It was the fall of 1994 and I was approached by a local police organization that wanted to illustrate their rescue dogs' ability to search for victims following a natural disaster. All the dogs were German shepherds, each trained to take a scent and then lead rescuers to the survivor's exact location. Such dogs are indispensable after a tornado, flood or fire.

The segment, which first aired live at 5:30 a.m., was staged at a huge limestone quarry and it began with the police squad's detailed explanation of their dogs' training. The police then suggested a demonstration where I would be buried somewhere in the limestone quarry to see if the three canines could find me. And how quickly.

I agreed. With one condition: I wanted Barney to be released with the other three dogs to see if he could find me, as well. I had no idea if he could. I didn't care. The great thing about my job is that it would have been great TV either way. Suppose he found me right away? Well, hooray for Barney. What a dog! Of course, maybe he'd have no interest in finding me and would just run off for a more appealing scent. Well, how funny is that? I couldn't lose, really!

Each dog got a good smell of me (sorry, I'm not sure how else I could have explained that), and they were then placed back in their cages while I hid far into the quarry under several large limestone boulders. Barney was also isolated so that all of the dogs would have to rely on scent and not visual cues to find me. I thought about blindfolding the dogs on TV, which seemed pretty funny at the time. But it was also pretty stupid, the police told me, so I didn't do it.

During the second live segment at 6:20, all three shepherds and Barney were released together. The rescue dogs headed to the quarry, each determined to find me. But they seemed a bit bewildered, smelling around everywhere, in a kind of sniff and miss manner.

Barney, on the other hand (paw?), was a dog on a mission. There was no perfunctory nosing about; he simply made a beeline to where I was hunkered down underneath a mammoth rock. He stuck his head down the hole and started wagging his tail.

TOTAL TIME: FORTY-FIVE SECONDS

The police were only mildly amused by this as I remember, although they did sing praises to the beagle nose, which has almost legendary status in the Proboscis Hall of Fame.

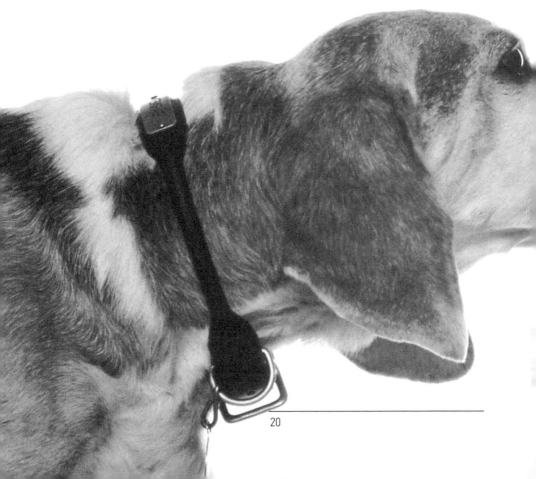

RAINMAN

IT WAS AUGUST, probably 1994, and it was State Fair time so all those years of corn dogs and deep-fried Twinkies kinda blend together in my mind, or what's left of it.

I was reporting from the annual hot air balloon race. There was always a great journalistic consistency to my coverage of the event. I would interview a pilot; he would tell me how safe ballooning was; then he would ask me to go up with him; and then I would chicken out. As the old adage goes, I was not afraid of flying; I was afraid of crashing.

This particular day was marked by rainstorms so torrential that the race itself would ultimately be cancelled. Barney and I had been camped inside the Channel 8 van staying dry and awaiting final word from one of the flight directors. I was distracted by a call from my producer and when I turned around, Barney was gone.

Most dogs do not like rain. Barney included. But this was the State Fair and already the aromas from the vendors had wafted toward the infield. I mean, beagles are only human. What could he do? He was off. At least I thought he was. Apparently, the severity of the rain had dampened even his spirits. What I saw next has become one of my favorite stories. I've told it a thousand times.

I looked out on the infield and saw a rotund man standing in a huge puddle of water. Apparently, he was in charge of the final decision as to the running of the race. I say rotund, but I am being kind. His potbelly protruded out almost a foot from his belt. But there he stood as the water cascaded down his rotund physique.

And Barney? His wanderlust had become a bit waterlogged, so he had situated himself between this man's legs, under his belly, using the man's girth as protection from the elements.

Every time the man moved, Barney repositioned himself. It was like a Kabuki dance.

When the rain stopped, Barney took off. I found him in front of an Italian sausage vendor. He was, of course, dry as a bone.

TIGER BARNEY Barney hated golf. But he loved to ride in golf carts. Here we are with Dr. Charles Poland at Brickyard Crossing.

BARNEY'S FRIENDS

COUCH POTATO BARNEY

A cooking demonstration at my house was cut short when Barney ate the plate of meatballs and platter of lasagna. Sweet dreams. Well, spicy ones, anyway.

THE DIARY OF CANNED FRANKS

DOGS LOVE TO eat. So do people. Most people are a bit more discerning than dogs. People don't eat things that will kill them. Unless you count elephant ears and deep-fried Hershey Bars, but it takes several years for those foods to work their terminal magic.

Some dogs will eat until they drop over and die. We see this trait in certain humans at the Golden Corral buffet, but overall, people know when to stop.

But beagles…beagles are a different breed. (You can't argue with that, can you?) Every time I talk to a beagle owner, they roll their eyes and recount an incredible story of how their beagle devoured an entire devil's food cake or a pair of pantyhose. One man told me his beagle punctured a can of pork and beans with his teeth. I don't believe that, but at least I got a good title for this story.

Barney was always hungry, but he was not stupid. He never ate a Frisbee, a package of dental floss, or a pot holder. He didn't have to—he could find real food anywhere. And half of Central Indiana had at one time or another fed him.

A few months after I got him, I took Barney on the Indiana Dinner train. It was part of a promotion we did with our Channel 8 viewers. This time it was a breakfast excursion. There were about one hundred people on the train and each had coffee, juice and a bran muffin. After the trip, I discovered that about fifty people never got to eat their bran muffin. Gee, I wonder why? That night I slept with a dog that had eaten fifty bran muffins. I'll spare you the details.

Some of the stories about Barney's eating have reached legendary status. You may have heard some of these, but I think you may find them funnier this time.

You've read about the huge pizza he inhaled and his sampling of the ant trap. Barney was so quick and smart, he always found food. But I did try to stop him. Really.

Whenever I brought Barney on location for the show, I went through a very thorough checklist before I let him run loose in someone's house or yard. I always asked three questions:

1. Is there anything around here he shouldn't eat?
2. IS THERE ANYTHING AROUND HERE HE SHOULDN'T EAT?
3. **IS THERE ANYTHING AROUND HERE HE SHOULDN'T EAT?**

For some reason, no matter how many times I said this, it always fell on deaf ears. The best example was St. Patrick's Day in 1996. We were doing a show at an Irish gift shop in Indianapolis. There didn't seem to be much in the way of food (not that something "in the way of food" would have stopped him), but I asked anyway.

1. Is there anything around here he shouldn't eat?
2. IS THERE ANYTHING AROUND HERE HE SHOULDN'T EAT?
3. **IS THERE ANYTHING AROUND HERE HE SHOULDN'T EAT?**

"Not a thing," said the owner. "Just gifts and clothing." With that assurance, I let Barney roam the store while the show progressed. In between segments, I saw the owner's daughter approach her mother. She seemed perplexed about something.

"Hey, Mom, where's that pound of butter that was on your desk in the back? We need it to bake the cookies."

"It must be there, sweetheart. Who would take a pound of butter?"

If I had had Irish blood, it would have been boiling. Yes, Barney ate four sticks of butter. Of course, I had to ask: "Didn't you say there was no food around he could eat?"

"Well, Dick, I never thought he'd eat a pound of butter."

"Did you think he was a on a low-fat diet?"

There is more to this story which continued as soon as Barney and I got home. You don't want to hear it. Trust me.

MY TOP TEN THINGS I HAVE EATEN

(AND LIVED TO HOWL ABOUT!)

BY BARNEY

1. Four sticks of butter at one time
2. An entire bucket of KFC
3. Half a turkey on Thanksgiving Day
4. An entire platter of lasagna (Garfield, eat your heart out)
5. Two packages of hot dog buns
6. A head of lettuce (I'll try anything once)
7. Two cherry pies
8. A box of chocolate cherries (Author's note: Don't tell me that's what killed him. This happened in 1993.)
9. A $20 giant pepperoni pizza (see story page 13)
10. An entire loaf of Italian bread (Well, not the whole loaf. I buried the rest under the blankets at the foot of Brett's bed.)

BARNEY AND BOOMER

Barney and Boomer made their own exercise video. The more Boomer sweated, the less he smelled like a cat. Barney was confused.

EATING CROW

"WE'LL BE HERE all day, said Dean Crow, a local videographer who was producing a TV spot for WISH-TV.

The script called for all the news anchors to play musical chairs. The segment progressed as an anchor was eliminated when the music temporarily stopped and—hey, do I have to explain musical chairs to you?

But the catch was that Barney was also supposed to play the game, hopping onto the vacant chair each time, leaving one of the TV anchors chairless. At the end of the spot, Barney was supposed to be the only one left.

"Yeah, yeah, very funny," Crow grumbled. "I hope I'm home in time for Christmas." (It was October.)

I didn't blame him for being a little concerned. Whoever wrote the script had a great idea, but just because it looked good on paper didn't mean we could pull it off. Dogs don't know how to play musical chairs. Do they?

Dean had not only underestimated the brilliant theatrical abilities of my dog, he had forgotten the persuasive effect of a hunk of pepperoni. Each time we did a take, the lead anchor cupped a piece of the succulent taste treat in his hand. Barney, of course, kept in close proximity as the Channel 8 talent paraded around the chairs. When the music stopped, everyone sat down, but the anchors always left an open seat next to the pepperoni purveyor. The dog never missed a cue. As soon as the chair opened up, Barney jumped into it, hoping for an opportunity to make a major salami score.

We did twenty or thirty takes, but few, if any, of those retakes resulted from Barney's failure to perform on cue. It was usually one of

The "Daybreak" crew in 2000 before a promo shoot. We were about to play musical chairs. Guess who won?

us or the camera crew who had goofed. These video people are very picky. Barney isn't. He'd have done his part for summer sausage.

If you watch the final TV spot that aired on Channel 8 (and I've watched it countless times in amazement), it looks as though we had rehearsed that bit a million times.

When we left, about an hour ahead of schedule, Dean Crow just shook his head. "I love working with animals," he laughed. "They're so much smarter than television people."

Dave Barras and Randy Ollis sit with Barney while shooting a TV spot. Barney liked Dave better that day. He had more biscuits hidden in his pocket.

STICKY PAWS BARNEY

Barney not only brought home the bacon, he stole it. As he did here while I did an interview at the Westin Hotel.

DINO MIGHT STORY

BARNEY CERTAINLY DIDN'T become a celebrity overnight. And the proof of that resulted in one of the most embarrassing moments of my career.

In the summer of '92, just months after Barney had made his debut, I was hired by the local Hardee's franchisee in Muncie to do a series of commercials. Part of the deal was a personal appearance on Saturday mornings when parents often brought their kids for breakfast and story time.

Convinced the kids would love the pooch, Hardee's did an extensive media blitz: COME MEET DICK WOLFSIE AND BARNEY SATURDAY MORNING.

In fact, those very words appeared on a billboard atop one of the Hardee's locations for more than a week.

I arrived my first Saturday morning almost an hour early. Imagine my delight to see a full parking lot and a huge line to get into the restaurant. "I am a hit," I thought to myself. "And this dog idea is brilliant!"

My elation was short-lived. The owner was making his way toward me. I expected a huge smile, but instead he looked as if he had just eaten a very bad cheeseburger.

"What's the matter? The place is rocking," I said.

"Yes, it is," came the response. "Now wait until the kids find out Barney is not a dinosaur."

The tail went between the legs—mine, not the dog's. Barney was ready to party. The parents were more disappointed than the kids.

I still think a real live beagle puppy is more fun than any stuffed purple dinosaur. Ask yourself this: Have you read Barney the Dinosaur's book? Oh, you have? Never mind.

CRUISIN' BARNEY

Barney could do lots of tricks. So could the photographers. It was very common to play with Barney's image. I wish someone would have done something with mine.

BARNEY THE BEAGLE

$100.00 REWARD FOR INFO
LEADING TO HIS RETURN

LOST AND FOUND

THIS BOOK COULD not have been written without some very special people. Not people who gave me emotional support; not people who helped me with the writing; no, not even people who loaned me money.

These are people who found Barney when he ran away from home and then called me to come and get him. It's a very long list.

During the first four years we had Barney, he ran away—wait, let me think—EVERY DAY.

Beagles are escape artists.

Barney would either get out the front door, the back door or the side door. He could go under the fence, through the fence and even over the fence.

He also jumped out my car window twice. He seldom came back on his own. Usually someone would find him and call. Those conversations reminded me of the great O. Henry short story, "The Ransom of Red Chief," when a couple of miscreants kidnapped an eight-year-old human bundle of aggravation, only to find that he was more trouble than any ransom was worth.

I'd scour the neighborhood with an eye toward open garbage pails or garages where the owners kept pet food. Sometimes, Barney would run off into the woods, but when he discovered that most food in the woods is still alive and required some form of pursuit, his interest in the forest waned.

His most famous escape would become a media event. It was about a year after he first debuted on TV and he had already become quite the celeb. I was upstairs working on a script when it dawned on me that I had not seen Barney for almost an hour. I hoped he had not gotten out.

This is not the kind of head start you want to give a two-year-old beagle.

I always used a very scientific approach when looking for Barney. I would drive my car to each street corner, open up my window and bellow his name as loud as I could. To call this form of search useless would be giving the plan too much credit. In all his years, he never came when I called him. Never. In fact, I am convinced that the sound of my voice assured him that I was nearby and that gave him the confidence and security to continue his journey.

Back to his most famous getaway: I searched for him for an entire week. I placed signs all over my neighborhood within a three-mile radius. The $100 reward generated a bit of interest—not quite like the $50 million for Osama Bin Laden, but in both cases the culprit was slippery and on the run. Whenever I got a call suggesting he had been spotted, I'd head in that direction with a photo and a glimmer of hope.

It did bring me into several, shall we say, transitional neighborhoods.

"Have you seen this dog?" I'd ask, flashing his photo to a group of young hoodlums…I mean, boys.

"Is he in trouble? What did he do? Are you a cop?"

"Hey, this is not 'Law and Order.' He's not in trouble. I just want to find my dog."

Every radio station in town was now asking their listeners to keep an eye out for a stray beagle. The term "stray beagle" is considered redundant by dog experts. I learned the hard way how many beagles had surrendered to their wanderlust and ventured out alone into a world chock full of enticing aromas. Over the six days, the on-air pleas and my ad in the local paper resulted in more than thirty calls from people who had either found or seen a wayward beagle.

Some of the calls were downright bizarre. People who had been on vacation in Florida called to tell me they saw a stray beagle at the Miami Airport or that they had seen Barney in a bookstore in North Carolina. I felt like the person in charge of Elvis sightings. People even called with female beagles, just in case I was confused.

I could dismiss most of the calls after a brief conversation. A description of his coat, his size and age were good tip-offs, but on several occasions, I needed to make a house call to confirm the identity of the dog. In many cases, the caller had simply seen a beagle in his or her vicinity, and while I did make a few excursions across town, I was pretty convinced that I'd never find him by combing a strange neighborhood.

And I figured he had to be close to home.

Boy, was I wrong.

The call came on the seventh day of his disappearance. It was a lady in Southport. "I think I have your dog, Mr. Wolfsie. I heard them talk about it on the radio."

"Well, that can't be. You live twenty miles from my house."

She described the dog. It sounded like Barney, but no way. Not Southport.

"What else can you tell me about him?"

"Well, he howled all day; he jumped up and ate our dinner off the dining room table; he sleeps right next to me; and he chewed my brand-new shoes."

After two weeks on the road, Barney returned. I put pins in a map where people claimed they had seen him.

"I'll be there in twenty minutes."

Sure enough, it was Barney. I was very happy. So was the lady who found him. She looked a little rattled.

It was Sunday afternoon and I decided to surprise the TV audience with his return on Monday morning during my segment on WISH-TV. That evening, the phone rang.

"Have you found your little friend?" an elderly woman inquired. "I've been so worried."

"Yes, I have," I beamed. "Aren't you nice to call. You can see us both tomorrow on TV."

"The dog is on TV?"

"Yes, of course. Isn't that how you knew to call?"

"No, I'm eighty years old and don't watch TV. But I saw your ad in the paper. Every Sunday night I call everyone who's lost a pet just to see if they found their little friend. Bye!"

The next morning, I did the show from my house. Barney made an entrance through my dining room doors. I could hear the cheers from the crew in the studio. I could feel the sighs of relief all over Central Indiana.

Did Barney really walk to Southport? Even I doubt that. He hitched a ride from someone, then took off when he had the chance. The lady who found him said he just appeared on her front step and howled to come in. That was Barney. He did not relish spending the evening outside in the cold. He knew he had to find a hot meal and a warm body to sleep next to. It was simply a matter of charming the pants off someone.

And he was very good at that.

IS THAT A DOUGHNUT I HEAR?

Rita Bordlemay outside her corn maze in Lebanon, Indiana. Barney had been lost in the stalks, but made a quick exit in search of a chocolate doughnut that he knew Rita was saving for him.

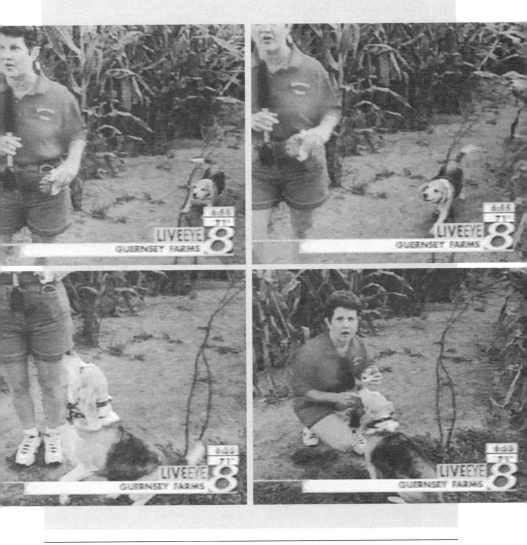

COMIC BARNEY

A caricature of us by *Garfield* staff cartoonist Gary Barker. I had ten thousand made. They're all gone but this one.

HE WORKED LIKE A DOG, SORT OF

BY LEE GILES, NEWS DIRECTOR, WISH-TV FROM 1970–2003

IT WAS ONE of those days on our early morning "Daybreak" newscast when a heavy snowfall was having its way with traffic, tempers, and disruptions of the routine. That's why Dick and Barney were out in the snow reporting on current conditions, instead of a normally pre-scheduled event.

I was standing behind the news producer and director in the control room with the two of them live on television when I got this inspiration. "Hey," I said, "have the photographer pan the camera over and show how deep the snow is on Barney." It was about "knee deep" to a dog where he was standing. But as the camera panned over, Barney began wading through the snow, as if he had his own earpiece and I was giving him directions from the control room. He kept going through several inches of snow,

News director Lee Giles takes down Dave Barras's photo and puts up Barney's. If he could only read a teleprompter. Barney, I mean.

belly high, then almost to his nose, so that you could see how deep it was. By golly, I thought, this is the way to report snow conditions.

You couldn't teach or direct that. And yes, maybe it was merely one of those totally timely coincidences. But I happen to believe that Barney simply had the natural instincts for good TV. I can't say I felt that way about every reporter.

And, my, did Barney have the gifts of patience, personality, and pleasure with children.

Kids could, and did, pet him, pound him, push and pull him from end to end. They shoved him, sat on him…sometimes a dozen kids at a time at personal appearances…and generally showed their love and attention to Barney as only kids can do. Barney never, and I mean never, let any of that bother him. He never fretted or even tried to walk away. He just "grinned" and took it for long minutes on end…better than any dog, or human, for that matter, could be expected to do. He truly seemed to enjoy it.

I'll always remember Barney in the midst of a group of Down syndrome children. He was sitting right in the middle of a very busy bunch of these youngsters, holding his head high, posture erect, letting the world know he was proud to be a part of this special time with these kids.

And just as he could smell out any food in the neighborhood, Barney also knew where his bread was buttered. Picture this: It's contract renewal time for Dick. He and Barney walk into my office. "Hi, Barn," I say. He looks me directly in the eye with an almost imperceptible nod, jumps up in the chair next to Dick, and we talk. For over an hour. Barney never moves, never howls (and boy, could he howl when he wanted), never does anything to disrupt these negotiations so key to his and Dick's career. When we're done, Dick and I get up and shake hands. Barney jumps down, looks me in the eye again, gives one wag of his tail, and if he could have talked, I would have sworn he was saying, "Thanks, boss, see you on TV."

A favorite photo. Barney and kids with Down syndrome. Somehow, he knew they were special.

STYLIN' BARNEY

A classic from "Daybreak." Makeover expert Jeffrey Bruce makes Barney into a French poodle. "A little more effeminate than I had planned," quipped Bruce.

DRUG DEAL

IT WAS A call from CVS Pharmacy headquarters in Wisconsin. I remember it like it was yesterday…

"Hello, may I speak to Barney Wolfsie please?"

"Excuse me?"

"Barney Wolfsie. Is he there?"

"Yes, he's here, but he's a dog. Do you still want to talk to him?"

(Long, LONG pause.)

"You say he's a dog? There must be some mistake."

"Well, I don't know whose mistake it would be. We both feel pretty good about the whole arrangement."

(Another long pause.)

"This is CVS Corporate and we're opening a new store in Indy. The store manager has a budget for a local celebrity to appear and he gave us Barney Wolfsie's name."

"Well, this is Dick Wolfsie."

"Hmmm…you don't seem to be mentioned here. Does Barney make personal appearances?"

"That's the only kind he makes!"

"I see. Would he be available on August 18th at around 2 p.m.?"

"Let me check my calendar . . . yes, we're available."

(Another pause.)

"Oh, do you go with him?"

I explained this again, and again, and again. I thought I had finally made it clear. Barney and I made our appearance and all went fine. Almost all. When I received the check from CVS Corporate, you guessed it: it was made out to Barney Wolfsie.

I put Barney's paw print on the back, countersigned it, and the nice people at Bank One cashed it for us.

BOUTIQUE BARNEY Barney was allowed anywhere. And he knew it.

BARNEY'S FRIENDS

GOING A LITTLE LOGO

EVERY DOG HAS his day, so the saying goes, but not every dog has his own logo. Once again, Barney was one of the exceptions.

The logos were not haphazardly slapped together. Oh, no. Some serious market research went into their design and production.

I'm not saying that these logos rival the Nike Whoosh, but . . . actually, that's exactly what I'm saying. These logos don't rival the Nike Whoosh.

The story begins with a call from Willow Marketing, a downtown Indy marketing and communications firm that had a really nifty promotional idea.

They were looking for the worst, that's right, THE WORST, logo in the Indianapolis market. Once determined, they would create a new logo for the "lucky winner," and profits for that company would soar. Or maybe they wouldn't soar. But who cared? It was a great idea for a promotion.

Brad Gillum, the CEO, called me just prior to the kick off of the campaign and asked if the concept might make a good TV segment on my show. I tried to hold back my enthusiasm as I imagined the perfect way to capitalize on this from a self-serving, self-indulgent, self-promotional point of view.

I was very good at that.

"Tell you what I'll do, Brad. Let's create a logo for Barney that I can use when Barney makes commercials. And we'll show that process on TV. It would help promote your contest."

"So, Dick, you want my company to make a free logo for your dog, so you can then market your dog and make money. That sounds awful-

The winning logo.

ly self-serving, self-indulgent, and self-promotional."

Man, this guy caught on fast.

But so did his artists, who ultimately produced more than a dozen options that captured the entrepreneurial spirit, the sales potential and the basic cuteness of my Barney.

But which one to choose? All had great potential. Take a look at the winning logo. Not everyone agreed with me, but I did think it portrayed the show-bizzy aspect of Barney. It was never officially used. But Butler Suzuki did proudly display it at their dealership.

WHERE'S THE BEEF?

BY STEVE SWEITZER NEWS OPERATIONS MANAGER, WISH-TV

THE URGENCY IN the firefighter's voice brought me scurrying from my tiny office. "We have flames showing with possible people trapped!" The emergency scanner in the WISH-TV newsroom usually offers an unending chatter that serves as the newsroom's answer to Muzak.

Dashing across the room, I notice Barney, our biggest TV celebrity, waddling in my direction. Normally, I'd take the time to scratch behind his ears but today, I only have time for a cursory "Hey, Barney." With the noon news quickly approaching, we know we'll need live coverage.

Barney wanders by with what I could swear is a grin on his face but the next half-hour is a frantic blur as the first crew on the scene advises that it's a huge fire. Over the scanner, a second alarm is sounded, calling in more manpower and equipment. We decide to break into the game show soon as we get live pictures from the scene.

The chaos doesn't let up until about 12:15 p.m. No one was trapped and the flames are turning to white smoke when I finally find time to think about something important: lunch. Today I'd brought a submarine sandwich piled high with lots of turkey and cheese packed onto home-made sourdough bread.

The first thing I see upon re-entering my office is Barney asleep on the floor. The next thing I notice is the baggie I'd carefully wrapped my sandwich in that morning. It is empty, laying a few inches from the snoozing beast's nose.

This wasn't the first time Barney had devoured my lunch. After all, he's a hound. He may not be much of a hunter but when it comes to food, he can sniff out an empty candy wrapper at the bottom of a trash can, a skill he'd demonstrated on several occasions.

"Wolfsie…" I bellow, "Barney's done it again…You owe me lunch from Shapiro's Deli." Dick arrives and pretends to scold Barney. "Bad Barney," he scowls, but both Barney and I know he doesn't really mean it. Dick never managed to sound convincing when he scolded Barney. That's why Barney was the master in their relationship.

Here we are on our way to Shapiro's for a replacement corned-beef sandwich. Nothing was Barney-proof.

Then Dick, as he had several times before, jumps in his car and goes to Shapiro's, bringing me back a scrumptious substitute for my original fare.

I'm not upset. Truth be told, my homemade sandwiches are okay, but I always looked forward to Barney's visit to my office. As Barney got older I left the food a little closer to the edge of my desk, and in his final years I left my lunch right in the middle of the floor.

When Barney ate my lunch, he was happy. I got a great lunch from Shapiro's. I was happy. We can only guess about Dick.

BARNEY LOOK-ALIKE CONTEST

WHAT'S THE FUNNIEST remark a guest ever made?

That's a great question. I'm really glad I asked it. And, as always, the answer involves Barney. That's why it's in this book.

It was the second Barney Look-Alike Contest. The first one was a fiasco, creating such chaos that I almost got fired. So, I decided to do it again. The first time we did it, people mailed in photos of their dogs and I picked the ones I thought most closely resembled Barney, who was then about four years old. Forty beagles showed up at Channel 8 studios, each one marking his or her territory. The 'his' marking is always more exciting than the 'hers' marking. Things were not only wet, but wild, as the dogs started crooning in unison.

Have you ever tried to stop forty beagles from howling? You might as well try to stop forty bulldogs from wheezing and drooling. Good luck.

When the show was over, I swore I would never do anything quite so hare-brained again. I should have put a Post-it note on my forehead, because three years later it was THE BARNEY LOOK-ALIKE CON-TEST II.

How could I improve on the first contest? That was easy. How about fewer dogs, more paper towels, ear plugs? This time I teamed up with Pet Supplies Plus, a local pet store that offered a five-hundred-dollar shopping spree as first prize. But all the entrants received a nifty gift package, worth about a hundred dollars, just for showing up.

I arrived at Pet Supplies Plus at five that morning and was elated to see about thirty-five beagles and their masters waiting for me. The aroma of the pet store had a stimulating effect on the hounds who were baying and spraying as only beagles can.

This was the last Barney Look-Alike Contest. If you had been there, you'd know why.

As I crouched to scratch a few beagle ears, the door of the pet shop opened and in walked a portly gentleman and his dog. Not a beagle—a bulldog. I walked over and bid the man good morning, then broke the news.

"Sir, this is a Barney Look-Alike contest. And that is a bulldog."

"Yeah, I know. So, I'll lose. Now where's my gift package?"

LETTERS TO BARNEY

OVER THE YEARS, Barney and I visited scores of elementary schools. Inevitably, the teacher would follow up our visit with an assignment to the class to write a thank you note to Dick and Barney.

For a long time, I just let the stack pile up, assuming that each letter was simply the requisite thank you and a sophomoric drawing of Barney.

Just before my first book *Life in a Nutshell* was published, I took the time to look through the close to two thousand letters that had accumulated in my garage.

Most of them were pretty perfunctory, but some were hilarious. Here are my ten favorites, some slightly edited, but all of them based on the kids' own words…

Dear Mr. Wolfsie,
Thanks for coming to our school. I would like to
watch you and Barney on TV, but my mom just lets us
watch stuff that is educational.

Kyle

Dear Mr. Wolfsie,
I love your dog. I think he is smarter than my brother.
Is he for sale?

Ernie

Dear Mr. Wolfsie,
Who makes more money, you or Barney? I have
watched you on TV and you should split it.

Effie

Dear Dick and Barney,

Thanks for coming to our school. Can you come for dinner some night? My mom would love that. I'm not sure about my dad.

Love, Kaitlyn

Dear Dick and Barney,

Thanks for coming to visit us. We were all very happy. Mainly because Mrs. Potter cancelled the test.

Lana

Dear Mr. Wolfsie,

It was very cool when Barney crawled on his belly when he wanted something. My father can do that.

Eric

Dear Dick and Barney,

My teacher said any of us could grow up to be like you, but just in case we don't, we should study hard.

Love, Toni

Dear Barney,

Thanks for coming to our school. And for bringing Dave with you.

Love, Erika

Dear Dick and Barney,

My dad said that you needed a dog to get people to like you. I really don't like dogs. Will a cat work?

Jona

Dear Mr. Wolfsie,

Where do you work? I see you on TV in the morning sometimes. But where do you work?

Anna

BARNEY'S FRIENDS

This was the set for Barney's Bad Movies. It was designed by producer Kim Gratz on a shoestring. The movies were purchased on a
shoestring. The staff was paid on a shoestring. We eventually got
the boot.

MOVIE MADNESS

I WASN'T ALONE in trying to use Barney as a marketing tool. Paul Karpowicz, the GM at WISH-TV in the early 1990s, had a few ideas of his own. One was particularly good. Although a bit weird.

Apparently, Channel 8 had a stockpile of old movies; some pretty good, but many clearly in the B-movie category. What did the B stand for? "Maybe it stands for 'beagle'," surmised Karpowicz, who suggested to me one day that we do a late-night movie show called—are you ready for this?—Barney's Bad Movies.

Pretty gutsy, really. We were advertising that the movies were stinko, but by putting Barney's name on the program, it might attract a bit more attention in that late night slot where ratings had waned on the weekends.

But wait. It was more than just the title for a show. We built this elaborate set with movie lights, an old movie projector and a dog house. There was a desk for me and a chair for the hound. This was real show biz. No expense was spared. That's because we had no money. We built the set from stuff people brought in.

Barney would have an actual role in rating the movies. For each film, we would pre-record what is called a wrap-around, TV talk for an intro and outro (yup, that's more TV talk) to the movie. Usually we'd make fun of the movie, but we'd always feature Barney in some quirky, off-beat way. If the movie was really bad, we'd take shots of Barney sleeping, usu-

ally on his back, and put them in the corner of the screen during the picture. Then when it was over we'd rate the movie with—yeah, you guessed it—one to four fire hydrants. Okay, so you didn't guess it.

Over the five-year run we even had special guests like Mayor Steve Goldsmith, Michael Medved, (the film critic), Boomer (the Pacers mascot), Comedian Soupy Sales and many of the Channel 8 reporters. Patty Spitler, the station film critic, made several appearances, often to defend the movie and spar with Barney over his fire hydrant ratings. Patty was much more forgiving.

The show lasted five years, but finally Barney lost his gig, the victim of poor ratings and the end of our rights to many of the movies.

That's show biz, even if you're a dog.

Barney's Bad Movies lasted five years. We didn't think it would last five minutes.

COMMERCIALS BARNEY APPEARED IN

(AND NOT ALWAYS WITH ME)

1. Palmer Dodge
2. Pet Supplies Plus
3. Suzuki
4. RHI Hospital
5. Uncle Bill's Pet Store
6. Your Man Tours
7. Hardee's Restaurants
8. HH Gregg
9. Fincorp sweatshirts
10. Blue Diamond Classics ('50s toy store)
11. Italiani's Restaurant
12. Meridian Music

COMMERCIAL BARNEY Ken Beckley and Barney. The spokes-dog and the spokesperson.

CLICK IT OR TICKET, BARNEY!

Barney does a Suzuki commercial. Someone e-mailed me and asked why he wasn't wearing a seat belt. At least he wasn't on his cell phone.

MY, HOW WE'VE AGED!

Throughout the years I signed and gave away thousands of photos. Many of the kids who got that first photo (far left) now have kids of their own.

PET SUPPLIES "PLUS"

WISH TV INDIANAPOLIS

Designed and printed by Image Pros at 2 N. Meridian St. Indpls. IN (317) 951-1665 / www.imageprosdigital.com

Barney

DICK
AND

ANAPOLIS

Dick Wolfsie & Barney
wolfsie@aol.com

WISH TV 8
www.wishtv.com

THE PICTURE PEOPLE

BARNEY BOXERS

IT ALL BEGAN with a phone call from a local manufacturer. He was looking for a little promotion for his sports apparel business, a business that produced a line of made-to-order clothing, featuring team logos and school names.

The guy wanted some free publicity, which was fine with me because that gave me an edge in asking for something extra to give the segment a little zing.

This time I really zinged the poor guy. I don't think he saw it coming.

"Tell you what," I said, "I'll do a show about your company if you'll agree to manufacture a line of underwear named after Barney."

His response said a lot.

"HUH?"

With that ringing endorsement, I went on to convince him this would be a great promotion for his company. The shorts would be priced inexpensively so our viewers would order on impulse. I don't think he ever expected the response that followed.

Three weeks later, we did a show from his plant, showing how a new product goes from design to

A brief reminder of Barney's popularity. We sold eight hundred pairs in an hour.

production. After the show, more than a thousand pairs of shorts were sold in less than four hours through the 800 number. His workers, who assembled the shorts by hand, would work overtime the next two weeks filling the orders for Father's Day. If you'll excuse a little underwear talk, it turned his business inside out.

I don't know how many men actually went to bed in Barney Boxers (a name that I coined and am damn proud of), but it is my guess that these shorts were all bought by women for their husbands, eager to put a little romance into their lives. Rumor has it that there was a minor baby boom nine months after the shorts were featured. I don't really believe that, but it's the only reference to sex in this entire book and I felt for sales purposes including it was very important.

BARNEY'S FRIENDS

HERE'S TO BARNEY

ALL OVER INDIANAPOLIS, things are named after Barney. There's a special place at Best Friends Kennel in Castleton called Barney's Suite Retreat. Pet owners still call and ask to reserve that unit for their pets. A sandwich at a local deli was named after Barney. It was all meat, no bun. There were the Barney Boxer shorts (see page 68). At one local eatery, Barney even had his own mini wine cellar. At the Humane Society, a dog log cabin bears his name. There is talk of naming a dog park after him.

But what would be the greatest testament possible if you were a canine? How about a drink named after you at one of the top restaurants in America: Ruth's Chris Steak House. Think of the honor. Patrons sip a very special libation bearing your name, before sinking their teeth into a $38 hunk of heaven.

No dog would turn his nose up at that opportunity. Except maybe a French poodle. Those French can be very snooty, you know.

Now Barney had already had one mis-adventure at Ruth's Chris, but he had apparently not worn out his welcome. In fact, they saw Barney's love of a good T-bone as a positive draw for their restaurant. Here's how the call went…

"Dick, it's Dan Forst from Caldwell VanRiper. We represent Ruth's Chris Steak House. As you know, we periodically name drinks after celebrities, like Mayor Goldsmith, and Big John Gillis. Anyway, we have a great idea."

"Why, Dan, do I think this great idea has nothing to do with naming a drink after Dick Wolfsie?"

"You're right on the money there, Dick. We want to name it after Barney. Isn't that a good idea?"

I couldn't see someone coming into the bar and saying, "Give me a

Barney." As with most ideas, it had potential. But Dan and I agreed that it needed a twist (so to speak).

The result was The Barney Name the Drink Contest, a proposition that almost drove me to you-know-what.

The first problem was getting permission to do this. Our then-general manager didn't like the idea. He thought it would be a mistake to associate Channel 8 news with drinking. (The news was already associated with murder, prostitution and plane crashes, but that didn't matter.) Beagles and booze were a bad combo, he said.

I explained to the GM that there was a drink named after Big John Gillis who did TRAFFIC REPORTS and Steve Goldsmith WHO RAN THE GOVERNMENT. They had no problem with this. Why did he? I found out the hard way that the GM felt no overwhelming obligation to explain his reasoning to me.

This really bothered me. I decided to go up to the GM's office the next morning, throw my con-

There was no alcohol in Barney's drink, but he would have liked Beefeater gin.

THE *Dick and Barney's* ALL BARK, NO BITE

CRANBERRY JUICE
VANILLA FLAVOR
SODA
LEMON TWIST

He's Barney the Beagle, Indy's most famous canine an the little chowhound gained immediate celebrity status whi wandered up on Wolfsie's doorstep nine years ago. Banis from the house for his destructive behavior, the troublesome took to the road to accompany his master every morning Channel 8. Dick and Barney have done some 6,000 live segments on Channel 8's morning news, Daybreak. Wheth Dick is wrestling a bear, sparring with Soupy Sales, or velcro himself to a wall, Barney is always by his side waiting for a tu or getting himself in trouble—whichever comes first. Barney represents a pet store and a car dealership. Barney even had his own TV show, Barney's Bad Movies, but it was cancelled. That's showbiz. Even for a dog.

ABSOLUT *Martini* SIGNATURE SERIES III

RUTH'S CHRIS STEAK HOUSE

The sound of perfection.

tract on the table and threaten to quit. My wife told me not to do this, so that was the end of that idea.

I tried one more time, suggesting that we name a non-alcohol drink after Barney. The answer was still no.

Then the saddest thing happened. The GM was fired. Oh man, just when I was starting to warm up to the guy. The new GM was Scott Blumenthal. I asked for a meeting to discuss this idea with him. The meeting lasted four seconds. Barney was going to have a drink named after him. Scott is still the GM. I'm sure this was his first great decision.

I decided to keep the idea of a liquorless drink, surmising that it would lend itself to some funny names, which it did. The contest lasted two weeks. The winner received a free dinner and assorted prizes. Here were some of the entries. They are a howl. Take a read.

K-9 KOOLER
BARNEY'S BONE DRY
PAWS THAT REFRESHES
BARNEY'S 8-BALL
BONE APERITIF
SHOT IN THE BARK
POOTCH HOOTCH
BARE BONES BREW
HAIR OF THE DOG
VIRGIN HAIR
ALL BARK NO BITE
TAIL CHASER
DOG GONE IT
BEAGLE JUICE
DESIGNATED WOOFER
RABBIT CHASER
HARE RAISER
BARNEY TEMPLE
BITELESS BARNEY
DOGGY DE LITEBONE DRY TWIST
BARNEY'S STRAWBERRY DOGAREE
DESIGNATED DOG
EARS TO YA

So, which name do you think won?
First, here are the ingredients. The drink was created by their bartender:

Cranberry Juice
Vanilla Flavor
Club Soda
Lemon Twist

The winner: BARNEY'S ALL BARK, NO BITE.
Here's to Barney!

DOG PADDLE BARNEY

Barney would do anything I asked (except come when I called him). He would also wear anything I put on him. And he never once complained.

LIVE EYE
I.U. NATATORIUM

SHOOTING STARS

BY CARL FINCHUM, WISH-TV PHOTOGRAPHER

WHEN DICK ASKED if I would like to write something about Barney for his book, I thought of all the escapades that would already have been talked about. As Dick and Barney's photographer for ten years, I remember all the antics: eating a whole pizza or a pound of butter; walking into a supermarket and stealing a chicken; sitting in line at a drive-up window waiting to be served.

But what I remember most was how Barney was Dick's pal. Barney put up with a lot. He was a foil for Dick's jokes, a partner in many of the segments, and an ambassador for when Dick went out in public. When Dick went to the RISE school, Barney hung around the special education kids. People always wanted to see Barn, but he had a sense of knowing when people really needed love—ladies at a nursing home or handicapped children. I think Barney knew what was really important besides a hamburger.

There was a reason Barney showed up on Dick's doorstep. Whether it was fate, karma, or Pluto aligning with Saturn, Barney needed Dick, and Dick needed Barney. They were pals, co-workers, buds. I used to joke that I thought Barn was reincarnated from someone. Someone who understood something that was more important than television. And that was friendship.

If a dog is man's best friend, then Barney was the greatest friend ever. Not just to Dick, but to everyone.

By the way, as photographer for Dick and Barney, I am often asked if he knew he was on TV. I don't think he ever fully understood that concept, but the dog was quite aware of it.

BARNEY BLURBS

MAGNETIC PERSONALITY!

IN TELEVISION, THERE is absolutely no jealousy among the talented people who are on camera. OUCH! Man, that hurts when your nose starts to grow.

Okay, there is some competitiveness, but no one would ever be envious of a dog. Would they?

Truth be told, I think everyone on the Channel 8 morning news got a big kick out of Barney's celebrity status. But I did put my good friend Dave Barras, the morning news anchor, to the test one morning. Dave was actually a very good sport about it. He probably should not have talked to me ever again.

Here's what happened: A local sign company, ATD Graphics, called and was looking for a little publicity for their shop. They made not only signs, but magnetic vinyl that could be affixed to cars for advertising and promotional purposes.

As I've mentioned before, conversations like this put me in a pretty good bargaining position because the caller wants free publicity (worth thousands of dollars) and I want a great show as well as something for my viewers.

With a bit of arm twisting, I convinced the folks at the sign company to send a free Barney refrigerator magnet to anyone who

Barney the Beagle!

DAYBREAK 8
W I S H T V I N D I A N A P O L I S
Dick Wolfsie & Barney
Magnets Compliments of
ATD 317-781-1640

Both Dave Barras and Barney had animal magnetism. But more people wanted Barney's magnet.

sent them a self-addressed, stamped envelope. Like the man who made the Barney Boxer shorts, I don't think this guy realized the response he would get. But he agreed to it.

After I hung up, I realized the idea needed tweaking. So tweak, I did. And here's what I came up with. We would make two magnets. One would have Barney's photo on it; the other would have Dave's. It would be a contest to see whose magnet would be more requested.

I called it a contest, but it was no contest. I knew it, the viewers knew it and Dave knew it. It was a massacre.

I will not give you the exact numbers out of respect for my buddy, Dave Barras. But in one way, Dave has saved face after all these years. His magnets are probably worth much more today than Barney's.

But that's because so very few were made.

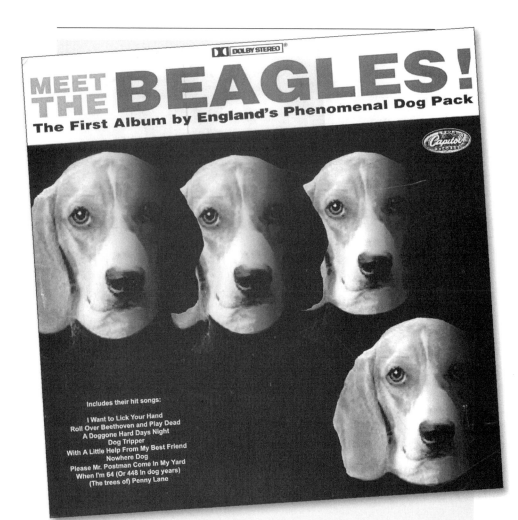

BEAGLE INVASION

The Knightsmen, a musical group that impersonated the Beatles, created this mock record album.

DUMPING ON THE COMPETITION

HERE'S ANOTHER LEGENDARY story, seen live on TV.

In the late fall of 1997, we did a "Daybreak" segment just outside the public relations firm Caldwell VanRiper on Meridian Street in Indianapolis. We were highlighting a sports mural that had been painted on the side of their building, showcasing the Indiana Pacers.

Right next door to Caldwell VanRiper is WRTV Channel 6, one of Channel 8's rival stations. Normally, I'd do everything possible to prevent their sign and logo being seen on WISH-TV. But as the live segment began, I noticed that Barney had roamed away from me and was sniffing along the grounds on the Channel 6 lawn.

What I saw next required an immediate journalistic decision, a decision that called into play all my experience as a broadcast professional. Should I tell my cameraman to pan over to the Channel 6 lawn and get a shot of Barney? Sure. Why not?

"Carl," I said, "Show the viewers what Barney thinks of the competition."

The camera pans: And 100,000 loyal Channel 8 viewers watched as my loveable beagle was seen squatting next to the Channel 6 sign and leaving a substantial reminder of his visit.

"How'd you get him to do that?" people asked me the next day. "We've been practicing for weeks," I said.

And I think some people believed me.

MUSIC TO HIS EARS

MY GUESTS ONE morning on Channel 8 had been booked at the last minute. When a segment cancels, beggars (that would be me) have to become choosers. But, as the adage suggests, we can't be TOO choosey.

Suffice it to say that the fill-in musicians I found needed to become a little more familiar with the concept of practice. I'm sure, over the years, they have gotten better. They must have.

When the segment started, the three electric banjos filled the tiny

Mexican restaurant with music. Well, as close to music as they were capable of getting. Three minutes later, things got better. That's because the first segment was finally over. But I still had one more segment to do. I couldn't hurt their feelings, so I knew I'd have to grin and listen to it.

Sadly, segment two started no better than the first one. But within ten seconds, there was suddenly silence. Inexplicable silence. The banjos were not working. The musicians looked at each other, fiddled with the electric cords to their banjos and shrugged their shoulders.

I was embarrassed for them but had no clue what to do. I walked over, explained to the audience that we had some technical difficulties and finished the segment just chatting with the guests.

What had happened? As the show ended, I walked around the corner into the next room. There was Barney with the extension cord in his mouth. He had pulled the plug from the socket. But he hadn't chewed through the cable; he had simply pulled it out of the wall—effectively ending the musical portion (thank goodness) of the show.

Even the musicians laughed when they saw what had happened. Of course, the whole thing was much funnier than they even realized.

GETTING A LEG UP

BEFORE YOU READ this story, I'm going to admit something. I'm not sure it's 100 percent true. I've told it for so long that I can't remember anymore. Vince Welsh, the sports director for WIBC can't remember either. But we think it's true. Most if it, anyway.

It was toward the end of the first year of Barney's debut. I had brought him on the show several times, but usually he would just be tethered to a stake (to a dog that doesn't know what a homonym is, this sounds like fun) adjacent to where I was reporting or doing my segment. To keep him in my view, I often attached him near the portable TV set that I used to monitor what was going on back at the TV station.

After one of Vince's sports updates, he was to toss it to me in the

URBAN LEGEND

With dozens of Indiana icons to choose from, *Indianapolis Monthly* editors chose a basketball, a race car, and guess who? for the cover of the *City Guide*. Barney made the cover twice. I never made the cover. Of anything.

field (this is sports/TV talk. Ain't learnin' fun?). Then Vince, who got a kick out of my bringing the dog on TV, asked about him.

"Where's Barney?"

"Oh, he's tied up over there by the TV set."

Vince couldn't resist…

"Well, he must be watching me. I guess he's a big fan."

At that point, Marcus, my cameraman, panned the camera to Barney who promptly lifted his leg and peed right on the TV set…

"Yeah, Vince, he's a BIG fan."

FOOD FOR THOUGHT

THIS STORY IS about Barney, but only indirectly. I shouldn't tell it because I promised my friend, Debbie Wilson of Gleaners Food Bank, that I wouldn't. Which shows you how much I can be trusted.

Debbie had called and asked that we do a show from Gleaners, promoting their food drive and encouraging people to participate by donating canned goods. Although everyone at Gleaners loved Barney, Debbie was unsure if health laws allowed me to bring the dog onto the food loading dock where we had planned to do the show.

Now Debbie used to be my producer when I did a talk show on Channel 13. We had a very interesting working agreement: She followed all the rules and I followed none. I think we were a good influence on each other.

So Debbie decided to call the Health Department to be sure we were not in violation of some code.

"Hello, Health Department? This is Debbie Wilson of Gleaners Food Bank. We're planning a show with Dick Wolfsie and I wanted to know if Barney was allowed on the dock with all the food?"

"Sure, why not?"

"Well, I thought we weren't allowed to have animals in the building."

"You have mice, don't you?"

(See why I went back on my word?)

GOURMAND BARNEY In the fall of 1993, "Daybreak" viewers took a ride on the Dinner Train. Here's Barney enjoying every minute and violating every Board of Health regulation.

VICE DOG

HERE'S A STORY captured on TV. Live. The guest in the studio was a Bill Clinton impersonator named Damien. That was his only name, so I don't know if that was his first name or last.

Anyway, he did a wonderful imitation of the president at a time when there was a LOT to make fun of, if you know what I mean. During one of the segments, Barney had jumped into the seat next to him and appeared to be quite taken with Damien's mimicry of the Commander in Chief.

At one point, Damien looked at Barney and launched into this long digression about how he was looking for a running mate and felt that

Al Gore did not have the personality to hold his own on the ticket.

The harangue continued for what seemed like forever. The whole bit needed a payoff—desperately. Finally, "Clinton" popped the question. "So Barney, would you like to be my running mate?"

Barney, who appeared to have been listening politely, if not intently, shot a glance at the president, let out a HUGE yawn, and jumped off the chair, leaving the president with a rather sheepish look.

Anchor Dave Barras could be heard laughing off-set. "We didn't rehearse that, I swear it," he was heard saying in the background.

Of course not. If we had rehearsed, it never would have happened.

ANYTHING FOR A LAUGH BARNEY Funny, he doesn't look Jewish! Barney at Church Brothers Collision Repair.

FRIENDS IN HIGH PLACES

Sandy Allen, the world's tallest woman, had a big heart. And Barney found a special place in it.

JOHN KLEIMAN

HOLLYWOOD STAR

IF YOU HAVE never gone to the Hollywood Bar and Filmworks in downtown Indy, you're missing out on a great evening. Watch first-run films and enjoy a meal and alcoholic beverages at your seat. Why buy a Coke for four dollars when you can have Budweiser?

Okay, okay, enough of the commercial. What does this have to do with Barney? Nothing really, but we got paid to throw this in the book.

Kidding! Kidding! Barney has played an integral part in Hollywood's success since 1997 when Ted Baltuch, the owner, asked if Barney could appear in a short piece of film that would introduce their full-length features.

In the video, Barney sits next to me as I explain to the audience

where the bathrooms are and the smoking policy of the theater. During my recitation, a big container of popcorn is placed in front of me by the waitress. For the next two minutes, as I struggle to continue my informative monologue, Barney stuffs his snout into the box and completely buries his head in the popcorn. "Leave my popcorn alone," I admonish him, but to no avail, of course.

Every time I visit the theater, I hear people laugh at that scene. "Does he really like popcorn that much?" they ask.

"No," I admit, "he actually doesn't like popcorn. It gets stuck in his teeth. But he loves Raisinets."

So what was the secret? Barney does love fried chicken wings, which were strategically placed in the bottom of the box.

And now you know the rest of the story.

Barney goes for my popcorn as part of the video that preceded every movie at Hollywood Bar and Filmworks. He actually didn't like popcorn. He liked the chicken wings in the bottom of the box.

BARNEY'S NANNY

BY MIKKI RANDOLPH, WHO STAYED WITH BARNEY WHEN THE WOLFSIE FAMILY WAS ON VACATION

"YOU COULDN'T WAIT until you got back to your own front yard?" I complained while scooping up what Dick Wolfsie called "celebrity poop." The early morning hour had contributed to my sleep-deprived, grumpy disposition, just five minutes into an intended burn-the-fat walk, necessary exercise for me as much as for Barney.

Barney looked at me with eyes that communicated, "I'm the best-known beagle in Indiana. What's the big deal?" Anxious for a new whiff of the next neighbor's mailbox post, he impatiently tugged at the leash as I struggled to twist-tie his aromatic gift.

I was Barney's nanny for twelve years. If it weren't for me, Dick and his wife would never have taken a vacation. They put Barney in a kennel once, but three days of non-stop howling by the beagle had resulted in a request by management to find other arrangements.

Barney operated on TV-time, responding to a 4 a.m. inner wake-up call, in eager anticipation of each day's "Daybreak" adventure. Barney had insisted I get out of bed hours before dawn even cracked. Finally, I acquiesced with absolute determination that today we'd walk briskly to honor Dick's charge to shape up one unshapely, food-obsessed, four-legged celebrity.

The words "Come on, Barney, let's walk fast so you can get a treat back home," did not deter the territorial beagle from spraying every hedge. Ever so slowly, this cardio-workout endeavor finally culminated in the two of us collapsed on the living room floor.

Barney delighted in snacks—so much so, that he developed a "quick leak, get a treat" routine. He'd race back in before the door shut, demand a treat, then beg to go out again to do his business, only to be rewarded once more. When the game met with resistance, he'd resort to pouting by jumping up on the couch and dislodging the pillows. "Do you want a treat? Okay, speak!" His barks produced the sought-after morsel. Then he'd cast a sly smile which said, "I won twice this time." Amazingly, his aging never decelerated his prance, his wagging tail, and his pure joy in treat-pursuit.

He adored company, especially when friends were invited for a meal. He refused to stay in his room, making sure that his protests interrupted any attempt at conversation. He'd approach every guest, begging for a sample of the current cuisine. If no response, he'd resort to the upright position of begging. How could anyone refuse such a gesture? Any wonder that a rounding belly was the subsequent outcome?

Barney loved to ride in the car, accustomed to a front seat view beside Dick as they rode to various "Daybreak" destinations. Dick's absence didn't dissuade Barney from expecting the same privileges during my visits. If left behind, Barney would convey his displeasure with deep, mournful wails.

Barney had his own room, adorned with his portraits by local artists and filled with gifts from adoring fans. He insisted that his dog bed be placed on top of a regular bed, but more often than not Barney would leave his bed in the middle of the night to nestle next to me.

He not only snored but audibly dreamed as well, having an occasional nightmare and emitting a growl or whine. I'd sometimes watch in amazement as his tail wagged, feeling certain that he must be devouring a pizza or another favorite non-doggy appetizer in his fantasies.

Taking care of Barney was never boring. To get my attention, he'd roll over, paws upright, waiting for a belly scratch. If ignored, he'd start scratching the carpet, then look to see if I was paying attention. He simply wanted to be petted and loved. That was his kind of exercise. Forget walking fast, forget low-cal dog food, and forget tummy-trimming.

Barney was one of a kind. An animal that penetrated hearts. A professional that loved to work. An entertainer that loved to make people laugh. An adorable beagle that enjoyed teasing his nanny. He leaves me many warm memories of a rainy dawn walk with a leash in one hand and Barney's "treat" in the other.

SHAWN SPENCE

GOT MILK, BARNEY?

The Girl Scouts loved Barney. Barney loved cookies.
Enough said.

A BITE ON THE RUN

Barney enjoyed catching Frisbees. Then eating them.

THE **TOTAL** **IDIOT'S** **GUIDE** TO

Beagles

10 QUESTIONS BEAGLE OWNERS ASK:

- How far back on the counter should I push the casserole?
- Where can I buy a 500-foot leash?
- Will duct tape keep the refrigerator door shut?
- Can you repair stuffed animals?
- Can I get my money back from obedience school training?
- What do I do when I say NO and the beagle says YES?
- What part of "Come here!" do beagles not understand?
- After how many days is a beagle considered legally missing?
- How can I say "Get out of the garbage!" and really mean it?

SPECIAL FEATURE
Stop your beagle from howling in 300 easy lessons

COLUMNS

During the twelve years that Barney appeared on TV, I wrote several news-paper columns about our adventures. Here are a few of my favorites. Some will make you laugh; some will make you cry. You'll know which are which.

BEAGLE MANIA

THIS COLUMN IS about my dog, Barney. He's not getting any younger so I want to make sure that I chronicle his short but incredible career. There will never be another dog like Barney, but of course we all feel that way about our dogs—and our kids.

Barney was a stray beagle. The words "beagle" and "stray" are some-what redundant. You see, beagles are really about 60 percent nose and 35 percent ears. Beagles don't just go out for a walk, they pack a suitcase. Beagles love to travel. The average beagle has more than 55,000 frequent flyer miles. As a result, there are lots of stray beagles. I did a brief survey once. Most people who own beagles either found them or were tricked into taking one from a friend. If you have a beagle and you actually paid for it, you need a good financial advisor.

Beagles are obsessed with food. Last Thanksgiving Barney ate four pieces of turkey. He would have eaten more, but he was saving room for dessert: two large cherry pies. We don't know how he got onto the dining room table, but we did learn one thing: He does have will power. When it comes to broccoli.

Several months ago my son and I were sharing a large pepperoni pizza when the phone rang. I retreated to my office, Brett to the TV. When I returned, the entire pizza had found its way into the beagle's belly. Panicked, I called the vet, thinking I needed to act quickly to prevent a dangerous medical emergency.

"Dr. McCune, it's Dick Wolfsie. Barney just ate a whole pepperoni pizza. What should I give him?'

"Gosh, I don't know. A Budweiser?"

I first met Barney when he wandered up onto my front step over seven years ago during the dead of winter. I placed him inside the house and went off to work. When I returned, there was hardly any house left. There were also no shoes left. He also chewed the eyes out of all my son's stuffed animals. "Can we NOT keep him," begged my son.

My wife was more direct.

"The dog is a menace. Get rid of him."

"What about obedience school?"

"Don't be silly. You're fully capable of doing what I tell you."

We did compromise. I got to keep the dog, but I had to take him to work with me every morning on Channel 8. And that's how Barney became a star. Now at age eight he is probably one of Indy's most recognizable personalities. Everywhere I go, people want to meet Barney, get his autograph, pet him and ask me questions.

Q. Is he really your dog?

A. No, he's actually a rental. In fact, the lease is up next month.

Q. Is Barney his real name?

A. No, his real name is Alan. Barney is a stage name.

Q. Does he get paid?

A. Yes, and he's in a 401K plan (the K is for kennel in case he wants to retire someday).

Q. He's not getting any younger is he?

A. Actually, he is. I expect in four more years he'll be a puppy again. By the way, you're not getting any younger, either.

Q. Does he mind getting up that early in the morning?

A. You know, he's never really complained, but last year he put his paw down about wearing makeup.

Q. Does he like being on TV?
A. Yes, but his dream has always been the movies.

Q. What will you do when he dies?
A. Stop bringing him on the show.

DOG TALK

FOR SEVERAL YEARS now, my dog, Barney, has been yapping about wanting to write a column for me. I have resisted this, but at the last Channel 8 Christmas party, Barney was given an award for ten years of service to the TV station. This has to be some kind of a milestone, not just for a dog, but for anyone who has the doggedness to stick with something for so long. Especially television. So, for this one time, the word processor is his. Go for it, Barney…

Thanks, Dick. First I want to say that Wolfsie and I have done almost three thousand TV shows together. That's nine thousand segments, and about twenty thousand guests. For ten years we have gotten up at 3:30 a.m.

and we have never missed a show by oversleeping. We are both dog-tired.

Once we get to our remote location, the fun starts. We have to organize three segments, be sure all the guests know their parts, check that all the names are spelled correctly and that my cameraman, Carl, has some idea what Wolfsie and I are going to do. All three of us work like dogs. Especially me.

On location, I usually have to do some kind of a segment that in some way humiliates me. I've been dressed as a woman, gotten pies in my face, been buried in a stone quarry, been covered with Jell-O, wrestled in the mud and worn funny hats. This is something that Channel 8 wants me to do. Sometimes I'd rather not. No one likes being treated like a dog. Especially me, again.

Wolfsie and I do try very hard to give you great TV because the other stations are always trying to beat us. The competition is very stiff, especially during ratings. Everyone's looking for the best stories and would do anything to crush the underdog. It's a dog-eat-dog world. Not very appetizing.

My job is fun. The hardest part is convincing people to be on the show that early in the morning. Lots of times Wolfsie and I have to do some serious cajoling and persuading. When people say no at first, we hound them a little bit. (That's my job.)

The executives at Channel 8 have always been a little wary of us. You see, Wolfsie and I do live TV. We never know what is going to happen or what we are going to say. There's a chance we could say or do something that would be very embarrassing and even get Channel 8 in trouble. That makes the bosses uneasy. So they watch us like dogs.

Usually the show is pretty good, but occasionally it's really amazing. In fact, sometimes Wolfsie comes home with an inflated view of himself. Every dog has his day, you know. Even humans.

Of course, sometimes the show is really bad. That's when we both get depressed. Then, Dick feels like dog meat. Sounds good to me.

But there are great aspects of my job. I get to meet interesting people, go to new places. Wolfsie and I have probably met more wonderful people in this town than anyone else in television. Hey, it's a dog's life.

One final note. Don't give Wolfsie any credit for making me a star. Quite the contrary. Before he found me I was already doing just fine, working the streets with my act and eking out a living. When I joined WISH-TV, I made Wolfsie the star. Talk about the tail wagging the dog!

Well, that's it. My column is over.

Doggone it.

Barney

WALK IN MY PAWS

I'M A LITTLE perplexed about all this interest in cloning your pet. No one should have a greater desire to do this than yours truly. After all, if it weren't for Barney, I could file the short form April 15th.

SPEEDRACER BARNEY Barney didn't lack the skill or courage to drive a racecar. He just lacked a booster seat.

AUTHOR, AUTHOR

Without Barney next to me I didn't sell many books. (I hope this book is an exception.) Here we are with Emily Hunt at a Marsh Supermarket.

But I'm against cloning. Who wants your pet back as a puppy or a kitten when the two of you have grown old together gracefully? I mean, would I want to come home one day and find my wife twenty-five years old again? Actually, I need to think about that one a little more. But I do know that I don't want a new Barney.

When I first got Barney eleven years ago, he was a year old and I was fortyish. He was neutered and I was married. I thought the similarity ended there. However, we did both look forward to our walk in the woods and after dinner we would bound out the door in search of a new adventure.

It's eleven years later. Both of us are now considered senior citizens and the walk seems more of an obligation. We both go, but I think the pooch would rather lie on the air conditioner vent and sleep. So would I. Unfortunately, Dr. Coss, MD and Dr. McCune, DVM both recommended daily exercise. So be it.

We usually start out at a good pace. I lumber for about twenty seconds, at which point both my heart and the dog's have reached peak cardiac rate. Both of us are about 15 percent over our optimum body weight so it isn't long before we're both tripping over our tongues.

By mutual consent, the three-mile walk is now just over a mile. In the summer, I bring a spray bottle when it's over seventy-five degrees and every tenth of a mile or so we sit on a rock and refresh ourselves. In the winter, we both bundle up, but within an hour all six of our feet are freezing and need to be rubbed.

We both have arthritis now and it couldn't have come at a better time. Seven years ago Barney would get the scent of a rabbit and take off into the woods. Even then, I couldn't keep up with a beagle pup. Now at seventy-seven, Barney still eyes the squirrels and rabbits, but knows that at his age he'll never catch one. He doesn't even make an effort anymore. Sometimes I'll eye an attractive young woman in the park. We then look at each other knowingly. Who are we kidding?

Both of us still enjoy the trees and wildlife, but we both have developed allergies to something in late summer, so it's not uncommon to see man and beagle walking down the trail sneezing and wheezing. In the winter, we both walk gingerly along the street, afraid we might slip and carom into a parked Chevy Blazer.

By the time we've walked about half a mile, Barney has relieved himself six or eight times. Even if I were inclined to do likewise, propriety (and having a recognizable face) prevents me from following suit. Nevertheless, I sense that when Barney is about ninety-one and I'm close to sixty we're going to require similar rest stop needs. We'll just walk deeper in the woods or I'll wear dark glasses.

As our walk comes to an end, we are both panting, looking forward to the ride home when we can both stick our heads out the window and let the wind run through our thinning and graying hair. Once we arrive home, Barney heads right for his bowl of cold water. I snap open a frosty beer and before long we are both napping on the sofa. That's usually when my wife gets home from work and thinks it's funny to point out that both the dog and I snore in perfect harmony.

It's not easy walking a dog when you're both getting up in years. If you must, start when your dog is two and you're fourteen. Enjoy it while it lasts.

SOUND OF SILENCE

(Although Barney was in pretty good health when I wrote this in October of 2002, his loss of hearing meant it was getting near the end. I didn't want to admit it. But I knew.)

BARNEY HAS LOST his hearing. Those big, floppy beagle ears that were once legendary are nothing but window dressing. How sad that is.

Barney could hear me crack a dog biscuit three rooms away. He could detect a wet noodle hitting the kitchen floor. He knew the doorbell was going to ring seconds before it chimed—he heard footsteps. When Barney was deep in our woods, I'd rattle a box of Milk Bones. He was at the back door in seconds.

No more.

I first suspected this was beginning just a few months ago. Commands like: Come here! Sit! Bad Dog! Stop Eating Trash! went unheeded. Of course, he never paid any attention to those commands when he had perfect hearing so I didn't realize fully what was happening.

PLAY IT AGAIN, BARNEY.

This was our first paid advertisement in 1993. Music to my ears.

For the past eleven years and three thousand TV shows on Channel 8, Barney has risen with me each morning at 3:30. I'd switch off the alarm, jump in the shower and get dressed. Waiting for me at the door half an hour later was Barney, ready for a new adventure. But one day recently, he wasn't at the door; he was still curled up in my bed, snoring away. He hadn't heard the alarm, or the shower, or the toilet flush. He was shaking and vibrating in the middle of some doggie fantasy dream. I hated to wake him up. But we had to go to work.

In the past, when the family would go out for the day, Barney would spend his afternoon on my bed, his head propped against my pillow, body stretched out in doggie heaven. But when we'd return, he'd hear the car pull into the driveway and dash downstairs to greet us at the door.

No more.

Now, I walk into the bedroom, where he is snoozing. I try to roust him by bellowing his name. "BARNEY! BARNEY, WE'RE HOME!"

No response.

I walk over and gently scratch his belly. His head snaps up like a jack-in-the-box. "WHAT IN BLAZES WAS THAT?" he seems to be saying. "YOU SCARED ME HALF TO DEATH." Like most dogs, and especially beagles, Barney was used to hearing it or smelling it before he saw it or felt it. Now I feel bad when I wake him. I feel like I should call home and say we're on the way...not that he would hear the phone.

Our walk in the woods has changed, as well. Beagles are hounds, bred to travel in packs when they hunt. Barney often walked ahead of me, but would on occasion twist his head around to be sure I was nearby, still part of the hunting party. But such confirmation was rare because he could hear my footsteps. On occasion, I would hide behind a tree. When the footsteps stopped, he predictably turned to check my whereabouts. This confirmed his devotion to me, a method that has never worked with my wife, who once walked ahead of me for three miles while I waited behind a tree.

My walk with Barney is different now. He doesn't hear my footsteps so he waddles along with his body almost at right angles, bent in the middle, so he can see me at every step. He looks as though he has a perpetual stiff neck. If he turns and looks ahead, he has no evidence I am following him. He has lost his radar.

Don't feel sorry for Barney. He can still smell a doughnut a block away and he remains bright-eyed and alert, even for thirteen. And people love Barney. Whenever they see him, they say: "ISN'T HE CUTE? ISN'T HE ADORABLE? ISN'T HE PRECIOUS?"

Yes, Barney has heard it all. But sadly, he'll never hear it again.

GOODBYE BARNEY

(I wrote this two days after Barney died. I cried for two hours as I typed it. I'm amazed I ever finished it.)

I LOST MY best friend this week. And my business partner. Barney was twelve or thirteen or fourteen—I never really knew his exact age. He was a street kid who wandered onto my doorstep looking for a better life. He found it. And I found the world's greatest dog.

I'm not going to tell you exactly when Barney died because after it

This is probably the last photo of Barney. He died six hours later. As you can see, he was happy 'til the end.

happened I lied to dozens of people. You might be one of them. "Where's Barney?" they yelled from their car the next day. "Home sleeping," I shot back. I didn't know what words to use. He wasn't just *my* dog that was gone. He was *their* dog. In many ways, Barney belonged to everyone.

When I walked down the street with him, four out of five people would say hello to the beagle by name. Many followed with a lame joke about not knowing my name. Sometimes they weren't kidding.

There was never another dog like him. He was a dog with many passions. People would joke that he looked like he hadn't missed many meals. I think he missed one, back in '95. He was endlessly hungry, relentlessly in a search for food he could steal. He ate everything: pickles, carrots, hot dog buns, tomatoes. And sometimes, when extremely desperate, he would eat his own dog food.

When he saw people approach in a mall, he rolled over on his back for the ultimate belly rub. If you stopped rubbing him, he glared at you. "You've got some nerve," he seemed to be saying. Everyone rubbed his belly—little old ladies, toddlers, Harley riders, even cat lovers.

As much as he loved me, he'd run away if he had the chance. Not run away from me, of course, but on to a new adventure. He knew I'd find him. Last Thanksgiving he got through the invisible fence and found his way to a holiday dinner several miles away. He barked at the unfamiliar door. He knew strangers were a softer touch at the dinner table.

Barney and I did three thousand TV shows together on Channel 8.

Barney knew television.

When a second-rate musician was playing his electric guitar on my show, Barney pulled the plug out of the wall with his teeth.

Barney knew music.

When the new Ruth's Chris opened downtown, Barney went into the kitchen during the show and stole a T-bone from the counter.

Barney knew steak.

When Barney was asleep, his tail actually wagged.

Barney knew how to dream.

When I did a show with kids with Down syndrome, Barney jumped on the bed with all fifteen toddlers and snuggled with them.

Barney knew how to love.

When I did a show with the Carmel High School baseball team, he stole the ball (and the show) and took off with the whole squad in hot pursuit.

Barney knew comedy.

When people took pictures of Barney, I swear he looked right at the camera.

Barney knew publicity.

Barney loved everyone. There were no strangers. I don't think he had an unhappy moment in his life. His final day was filled with good food and adoring fans. That evening he passed peacefully in his sleep.

Barney even knew how to die.

Over the years, I have given out over five thousand photos of Barney, each inscribed by me with a silly facsimile of a paw print. If you have a picture of Barney with that paw print, please keep it in his memory. That would mean a lot to me.

And, I am sure, it would mean a lot to Barney.

ONE MORE GOODBYE

THIS PAST WEEK has been a tough one. I didn't love my dog a woof more than you love your pet, but Barney was also adored by tens of thousands of others. Normally, I enjoy the spotlight that TV and my writing provide me, but the public grieving that ensued after Barney's death has been a double-edged sword.

At last count, I had received over 1,100 e-mails. Of course, I read each one and began an attempt to answer each of them. But the task is Herculean.

I experimented with a generic thank you that I could cut and paste and send back, but the very act seemed insensitive. People had spent a fair amount of time sharing their memories of the beagle, so my techno-approach seemed a disservice to Barney's fans. I'm still struggling with how to deal with all the wonderful people who sent their regards.

The day after Barney died, every single newscast in Indianapolis covered his passing. Anchors Debby Knox (left) and Pam Elliot (above) were both touched by Barney's passing.

Please don't send me any suggestions. My hard drive is in a bit of a snit as it is. But please know how much I appreciate your thoughts.

Here are a few observations based on my slew of e-mails, as well as letters and phone calls:

1. Many people sent their condolences, but hundreds also remembered specific shows that even eight to ten years later were fresh in their minds:

> The time he ran away.
> The time Barney howled at me in the glider.
> The time he chewed up the boxing glove.
> The time he stole and ate four sticks of butter.
> The time he found me buried in a quarry.
> The time he got a therapeutic massage.
> The time he got a manicure.
> The time he tried to herd sheep (and wandered off in the woods).
> The time he dug up the garden.

The list is endless. I wish I had saved each show on videotape. I didn't, so these memories are especially important to me.

2. Even more people had memories of meeting Barney in person. Inevitably, Barney was either eating something he shouldn't have been or had rolled over on his back to be belly-rubbed. But here's my favorite, slightly edited:

> Last year, I took my two nieces to the Gift and Hobby Show to see Santa Claus. That evening the Santa booth was deserted. Brittnee was devastated and cried and cried. Then she saw you and Barney. She stopped crying, ran to Barney, sat on the floor, and petted him. That night, Barney meant more to a five-year-old than Santa Claus. The next day, she told her grandma that she saw Barney and got his autograph. On Monday, she took the photo to kindergarten. Her autographed photo is still proudly displayed on her bulletin board in her room.

3. Is there a heaven for dogs? About seventy people assured me

Posted outside a veterinary clinic in Westfield. They never treated Barney. They just loved him.

there was and I would see Barney there someday. I'm not totally sure what the criteria are for heaven. I just hope we end up in the same place.

4. People had opinions about whether I should get another dog. Should it be a beagle? And should I name it Barney? Opinions were mixed, many saying that "Dick and Barney" was a moniker that should remain intact. Others felt it would be easier for me emotionally NOT to have a dog that looked like Barney and shared his name. And it would keep his memory distinct.

I don't know what I am going to do. I am taking a breather for a few weeks to think about this. One thing is sure: The dog must have a temperament like Barney's. And a personality that comes across on TV. Not easy to find.

5. And, finally, people wanted to know about the final arrangements for Barney. The weekend before he died I took my family to the movie *Seabiscuit*. As you will see on page 127, seeing that movie influenced my decision.

My favorite photo of Barney, taken by WISH-T Photographer Bill Fisher.

ANOTHER DAY, ANOTHER DOG?

HOW OLD IS Barney? I used to answer that question a hundred times a day. Now that the little mischief-maker is gone, the query I get most often is: Will there be another Barney?

When I first went on TV to tell the public that Barney died, I made the mistake of saying, "Yes, there will be another Barney, and, yes, his name will also be Barney."

I'm not sure what moved me to say that. No doubt my sadness and the feedback from consoling people motivated me to jump the gun a bit. I wish I had given it some more thought.

No, there will NOT be another Barney. Not for a while anyway. "But what about a different dog?" people will no doubt ask. "Maybe a poodle or a Rottweiler?"

Keep in mind that I never planned to put Barney on TV. He wandered onto my doorstep, a hapless stray, and after destroying the house, my wife banned him from a few rooms: bedrooms, bathrooms, kitchen, great room, basement, and dining room. Other than that, he could go anywhere he wanted.

Barney did not like the laundry room, so I took the pup to work with me. It was never my intention to make him a star, to produce a celebrity canine, or make a buck off the pooch. It just happened.

I guess I had forgotten that. And that's an important part of the story. Some things in life you can't re-create. My grandmother never wrote down the recipe for her spaghetti sauce. Why? "Just because you put the same ingredients in doesn't mean it will taste the same," she used to say. I never really understood that. Now, I do.

Over the past month, I have gone to visit about a dozen beagles needing new homes. My heart wasn't really in it. I felt like I was looking for a used car. Will he howl? Will he get into trouble? Will he steal food? Will he get into the garbage?

Many of the beagle owners swore their dogs would not do any of this—which was too bad, because that was exactly what I was looking for. Barney had personality, too much at times, but that was what made him a star. Even when he was sleeping, he looked like he was dreaming up trouble.

There is a part of me that feels a bit insecure about the whole situation. I used to laugh when people said he was more popular than me. It doesn't seem quite as funny anymore.

Was I jealous of Barney? Of course I wasn't jealous of a dog. But I also knew if there was a crowd of people around Dick Wolfsie, it was really a crowd of people around Barney. That was okay with me. "I get to cash the paycheck," I would often quip. But few other Channel 8 personalities were offered as many opportunities to interact with the public as I was. I mean, as WE were.

So, I'm on my own. I think I can make it. Sometimes, I think if I had droopy eyes, a forlorn face and a fat belly, I'd be more popular. Of course, I'm fifty-six now and who knows what the future will bring?

DOG GONE LIAR

I'M A LIAR. A big fat liar. But a well-intentioned one.

I wrote a few weeks ago that there would not be another Barney. At that time, I was going back on a promise I originally made when I said on TV there would be another Barney. In a way, I lied twice, which brings me to the truth.

If you don't have the foggiest idea what I'm talking about, I don't blame you. If you think I have a career in politics, you may be right.

Here's the bottom line: I have a new dog and his name is ( ). I am not going to tell you his name because he was a stray and he had a collar. When the nice lady who found him called the owners, they said they didn't want him. So she called me and I went over and met ( ). I didn't think I could fall in love again. Go figure.

( ) is a beautiful two-year-old male beagle, completely housebroken and the sweetest thing this side of peach iced tea. But his owners said, "You can have him."

So the reason I'm not telling you his name is that if these folks realized I had ( ) they might want him back or they might be annoyed that I gave them a hard time in my column for abandoning him. If you see me in person, I'll tell you his name. But I won't print it in the newspaper.

( ) won't be on TV with me. I've decided that because I have some

( ) and me. He has big paws to fill.

LETTERS

Barney's death prompted 1,700 e-mails and letters. I read every one. I wish I could have answered them all.

new assignments at Channel 8, it would be better just to make him my personal dog. Oh, he'll accompany me when I make appearances and you might see his head sticking out of my car window, but that's about it. I think I'll keep ( ) out of show business.

The one problem has been our cat, Benson. When ( ) first walked in the house, Benson thought ( ) was Barney. Benson and Barney were never soulmates, but they co-existed peacefully. Once Benson got a whiff of ( ), his hair stood up and he had a mini-tantrum. ( ) wanted to play, but Benson was not happy sharing his territory with an intruder. Right now they are upstairs staring each other down. I can hear Benson, who is about one-fifth the size of ( ) and eighteen years older, hissing away, protecting his turf. Never underestimate a clawless twenty-year-old cat who still catches mice. That's why we call him Crazy Old Benson.

My wife is already fond of ( ), although it disturbs her that ( ) doesn't have perfect manners. It also disturbs Mary Ellen that I don't have perfect manners, but I'm betting that we can both stick around for a while.

My sixteen-year-old son, Brett, is taking a little longer to warm up to ( ). Brett says the dog's misbehavior should not be tolerated. Let me repeat that so we can all have a good laugh: My sixteen-year-old, adolescent, teenage son says that misbehavior should not be tolerated. Sorry for the redundancies, but I think you get my point.

Well, wish me luck. I hope I see you out and about. If I do, I'll tell you ( )'s name.

TALKING TRASH

SEVERAL YEARS AGO, I wrote a piece about how to train your dog. I knew nothing about this activity, but I see lots of people writing about things they know nothing about… so why not me?

Just to review, here were a few of my suggestions:

1. When training a dog, use American cheese. Why? Have you ever tasted a dog biscuit? Sure you have. Would you roll over for one?

2. Always say your dog's name before you give him a command. For

example: "Winston, roll over!" Or, "Chivas, heel!" If your dog has a common first name, use his last name to avoid confusion. "Fido Bernstein, sit!"

3. Do not raise your voice to discipline. Did it work for your kids? Do you want a dog that behaves like a teenager?

4. Do not teach your male dog to shake. Every dog can do this. Teach your female to curtsy and you're looking at a trip to the Dave Letterman show.

5. Never buy a book called *How to Train a Rottweiler*. Use your old book, *How to Train a Poodle*. It's the same book. They just changed the photos. Same with *How to Train Your Hermit Crab*. Buyer beware.

These were just a few of my suggestions, but that was years ago. Now I have a new dog and I would like to advocate a unique system that I call the hands-off approach to dog training. I am convinced that it NEVER makes any sense to hit your dog. Even a tiny bit. Here's why:

First, imagine that you are a dog. Come on, try harder. Give yourself some floppy ears and a wet nose.

Isn't that cute?

Now imagine you are a beagle, obsessed with food, always in pursuit of your next meal. Great. Now let's hear you howl. I can't believe you're doing this. What's this? Someone has left the garage door open. Quick, sneak inside. Now jump up on the garbage pail and tip it over.

Good job. Now, sniff, paw, and stick your head inside. All the way in. Oh joy, a half-eaten burrito. Quick, eat it. DEEEELICIOUS. Uh oh, here comes your owner. He screams: NO, NO, NO. BAD BAD BAD DOG! You're beginning to think that's your name.

Then, he takes a swat at your rear end. Not too hard, of course. He loves you. He doesn't want to hurt you, he just wants you to remember that this is inappropriate behavior.

And, you will remember. But what you will remember is that fragrant burrito. That piquant sauce, the succulent ground beef and the luscious cheese.

So, the next day, you're back in the garage. This time the unmistakable smell of a cheeseburger's last few bites fills the air. You think to yourself, "Okay, I may get caught rummaging through the trash. My master will yell at me. Then he will swat me on the tush. Is it worth all that just to get a few bites of cold cheeseburger?"

I ask you, beagle impersonators, what do you think? Is it worth it? Well, you can bet your beagle ears it is. Enjoy. And don't forget the soggy French fries at the very bottom of the garbage pail.

A final word about doggie discipline. And I'm sure you've heard this advice before. It's always best to keep a lid on it.

THE FINAL GOOD-BYE (REALLY!)

I did not want to write this final article for the December 2003 issue of Indianapolis Monthly. *It was three weeks after Barney died and I was beginning to get over my initial shock. My old friend, Debbie Paul, editorial director (and former editor), had put Barney on the cover of her magazine three times. It was hard to say no to her. And in my heart, I knew I still had a little left to say. I'm glad I wrote this.*

"IT'S BARNEY," MY wife said over the car phone. "There's something wrong."

"I'll be right home." I sped through the streets of Castleton. The cell phone rang one more time.

Mary Ellen again: "Don't have an accident. It's too late. He's gone. Barney is gone."

I banged my wrists against the steering wheel. I wanted it to hurt. I wanted to feel something. I couldn't find the tears. Not yet. I remember saying "Oh, God, Oh, God. Oh, God."

How odd to talk to yourself like that. Even then I knew how strange it was. My life is performing in front of people. But no audience here. Just me. In a car. Alone. I was still ten miles from what would be one of the most difficult moments of my life.

I shot into the driveway, slammed on the brakes and barreled up the stairs. I'm not sure why I hurried. It was over. The inevitable had happened. Barney the Beagle, my best friend, my business partner, had died.

I picked him up. I buried my head in his neck and wailed. My son, Brett, had never seen me cry. I think it frightened him horribly. I remember the first time I saw my father weep. It made him seem more

Barney's grave. Rest in peace, old pal.

human. I wondered how Brett would remember this.

I didn't love my dog a woof more than anyone else loves his dog. But here's the difference. Barney was not my dog; he was everyone's dog. This is not just romantic notion of mine. I have the proof.

In the weeks that followed, I received over 1,700 pieces of correspondence, which included over 1,100 e-mails, 400 letters, and a dozen bouquets of flowers.

I even received phone calls from complete strangers:

"Hello, Mr. Wolfsie. This is Eileen Patterson from Tipton and I, I …."

"It's okay, it's okay. Stop crying. Just take a deep breath. Hey weren't you calling to make me feel better?"

Each letter had a specific memory of something Barney had done—and probably shouldn't have done. The time he ate the catcher's mitt; the time he was on top of the diving board; the time he ate four sticks of butter; the time he stole the sirloin steak; the time he howled along with the *Star Spangled Banner*; the time he was in the drive-in lane at Hardee's waiting for it to open.

Many of the letters were about personal contact people had with Barney—the time Barney got in my purse; the time he ate my son's ice cream; the time my daughter petted his belly; the time Barney snuggled with the entire Girl Scout troop…

Here's a favorite:

Dear Dick,

I cried when I heard about Barney. But not as much as my daughter did. She is sixteen now, but when she was five, she was very afraid of dogs. At the Boat Sport and Travel Show, Barney crawled over to her on his belly, rolled over on his back and sneezed. My daughter started to giggle and couldn't stop. She has loved dogs ever since.

And one more:

Dear Mr. Wolfsie,

Last year, I took my two nieces to the Gift and Hobby Show to see Santa Claus. That evening the Santa booth was deserted. Brittnee was devastated and cried and cried. Then she saw you and Barney. She stopped crying, ran to Barney, sat on the floor, and petted him. That night, Barney meant more to a five-year-old than Santa Claus. The next day, she told her grandma that she saw Barney and got his autograph. On Monday, she took the photo to kindergarten. Her autographed photo is still proudly displayed on her bulletin board in her room.

"He was such a good dog," many people wrote, which wasn't true at all. Barney was actually a bad dog. But bad in the most charming and alluring way. He was the mischievous little part of all of us. Nothing sinister, nothing malicious, just forty pounds of trouble. He was hard to pick up. But he wasn't hard to love.

The camera especially loved him. As I sat and watched hours and hours of video tape, I was struck at how often he would do something totally outrageous. Totally unpredictable. Totally funny. Can a dog have a sense of humor? Barney did. I'd swear that dog knew comedy.

Once during a WISH-TV segment at the Caldwell Van Riper advertising agency on Meridian Street, the camera panned to Barney who had wandered next door and was doing the proverbial squat on the lawn of WRTV, right in front of their sign. "He was never a fan of the competition," I quipped. (I do get some credit for writing his material.)

Prior to Clinton's second run for the White House, an impersonator of the president visited our studio. Barney sat next to him during his performance. "I'm looking for a running mate," the actor said, turning to Barney. "I wonder if you'd be interested." Barney yawned, shook his head, and jumped off the couch. That dog had timing.

Barney's final week was spent at the Indiana State Fair. One morning, the Westin Hotel was demonstrating their new Heavenly Bed for Dogs, part of a new campaign to promote traveling with your pet. Barney took his cue, as always. He climbed onto the bed, offered his signature howl, then rolled over and went to sleep on his back. "If that performance had been for sale," said the hotel manager, "I don't think we could have afforded it."

It was fairly hot on Barney's final day at the fair and that may have been too much for a thirteen-year-old dog. I felt a great deal of guilt for over a week. I now realize this is how Barney would have wanted it. Barney had been to every State Fair during his thirteen years.

That day he helped me sell books at the Gazebo, howled at people for their corn dogs and rode in the celebrity parade. As the tractor passed by with Channel 8 personalities like Steve Bray and Twila Snyder, and a bunch of radio DJs, only one name was chanted repeatedly:

BARNEY!

HI, BARNEY!

HEY, THERE'S BARNEY!

I'd swear he knew it was all about him. It always was. And he loved every minute of it. If Barney could have planned his last day, it would have been at the State Fair: fifty-thousand people, twenty-thousand smells. He didn't have to die that day. He was already in heaven.

Every year, Governor Frank O'Bannon came over during the fair's

BARNEY STUFF

My entire room is filled with "Barney art." Here are two favorites: a wire sculpture by Bill Arnold and a pencil sketch by Deborah Downey De Fazio.

balloon race and scratched Barney's ears. This year was no different. Sadly, it was the last fair for both of them.

And here's a part of the story I have never told anyone. The day after Barney died, I went to work as usual. I couldn't cancel the show. I tried so hard to hide my grief. Not a chance. Howard Helmer, my old friend, and the world's greatest omelet maker, was the guest. "Are you okay?" he asked. "You seem distracted." I waved it off. "I'm fine, thanks," I said.

Later that day, an e-mail from Howard: "I'm worried about you. Are you SURE you are okay?"

I wasn't. I kept telling myself that Barney wasn't dead…just sleeping again. Incredibly, that seemed to help. I still tell myself that. Whatever works.

I did not reveal Barney's death until the following week. I needed time to decide how to handle it. I couldn't talk about it. I knew that people would be sad, but the response was overwhelming.

When Amali the elephant died, the zookeepers wept. So did more than a few who had visited the zoo and watched the huge creature from afar. But Barney was in your living room each morning. Then you could walk out the door and see him somewhere on location, rub his belly at the State Fair, or feed him a treat at one of our station events. If you saw me at the supermarket, you could come out to the car and scratch his ears and get a photo. You could see me walking Barney in the woods or say hi to us at a book signing in a mall. At traffic lights, people would crane their necks to see if he was with me. He was. Almost always. But he was usually asleep.

Two questions I have been asked countless times: Where is Barney's final resting place? And, will you get another dog?

I took my family to see the movie *Seabiscuit* the weekend before Barney died. Seabiscuit was a horse whose spirit captured the imagination of the entire country. When Seabiscuit died, people mourned. Seabiscuit's owner, Charles Howard, never revealed to the public his horse's final resting-place. To use some equine terminology, I think I'll take his lead.

Will there be another Barney? My answer the first week after his death was a resounding YES. I even promised this on TV. But now the answer is a howling NO.

Barney was never planned as a publicity gimmick or a ratings booster. He was a little bandit who found his way onto my doorstep. His manners were so atrocious that my wife banned him from the house. Her legendary words: "If you want to keep that dog," she said as she looked down at six pairs of shoes that had been chewed to bits, "take him to work with you."

Thank you, Mary Ellen. Thank you, thank you.

No, I didn't put Barney on TV, he just kinda sniffed his way onto the set one morning while I was doing the show. The response was immediate. People adored him. Such a happenstance can never be re-created. Barney was so unique, so special, that he actually made people feel good. Going on the air with another dog would be nothing more than a transparent attempt to capitalize on that once-in-a-lifetime confluence, a word I don't use lightly. Or very often.

When I think about Barney—and I do every day—I have one enduring vision in my mind. It was the day we visited Emily Hunt, the little girl tragically paralyzed at Old Indiana Fun Park in a train-ride accident.

Emily was not a morning person. Physically and mentally, it was tough to gear up for the day, especially when we needed her to be bright and cheery at 5:45 a.m. "You can expect quite a scowl," Mike, her dad, predicted. It's not easy interviewing someone with a face as long as Seabiscuit's. I felt guilty for intruding. With that, Barney jumped onto the bed and rolled his big brown eyes at her. If ever there was a smile that lit up a room, it was Emily's.

Mike Hunt recently sent me that photo. And this is now the one I treasure most. This is what Barney was all about. Take a look at it. And then you'll know why there will never be another Barney.

EMILY AND BARNEY

Barney with Emily Hunt. He made her smile. Even at 6:00 a.m.

BARNEY'S PROFILE

TRI-COLOR HOUND

BORN:
Circa 1990

LOCATION:
Unknown

FOUND:
February 1992
in Meridian Kessler area

DIED:
August 2003

NUMBER OF SHOWS ON WHICH
HE ACCOMPANIED DICK:
Approximately 3,000

NUMBER OF COMMERCIALS HE STARRED IN
17

AWARDS:
Beagle of the Wabash and the Poodleitzer Prize
(just kidding)

FAVORITE DOG FOOD:
Iams, at first. Then in his later years, a prescribed food
for his kidney problem. He would only eat it if I put
chicken or beef consommé soup on top.

FAVORITE CAT FOOD:
Whatever the cats were eating

FAVORITE CHEW TOY:
Rawhide bone (there were dozens buried in the yard)
and my eyeglasses (thank God for readers
at the dollar store)

FAVORITE SNACK:
Pupperoni (it's very good—I even tried it)

LEAST FAVORITE SNACK:
Broccoli (but he still ate it)

FAVORITE PEOPLE:
Mikki (his nanny) and Bonnie's Maids

FAVORITE PLACE TO WALK:
Near Geist Reservoir

FAVORITE PLACE TO VISIT:
Indiana State Fair, Broad Ripple Dog Park,
the trash cans in our garage

LEAST FAVORITE PLACE TO VISIT:
Market Square Arena. He slipped on the ice once and
was scared to go back. He was happy when they tore it down.

BEST TRICK:
He could crawl along on his belly the whole length of a room.

WORST HABITS:
Rubbing his butt against the couch, snoring, jumping up on
the dinner table (oh yeah, and rolling in geese droppings)

FAVORITE PLACE TO SLEEP:
In his bed (on top of my bed), often on his back, usually
after rolling in geese droppings

FAVORITE PASTIME:
In the summer, hanging out on the front lawn. In his
later years, he let the wind bring the smells to him.
And rolling in geese droppings.

FAVORITE COSTUME:
My favorite was the Harley biker outfit. I wish I knew
how he felt when I dressed him in stuff like that.
He never complained. He never said anything.

FAVORITE SHOW:
Spent a morning at Ruth's Chris Steak House (DUH!)

VETERINARIAN:
Dr. Bob McCune, Stoney Creek Pet Clinic

NANNY:
Mikki Randolph

PHOTOGRAPHERS:
Marcus Collins
Carl Finchum

FAVORITE QUOTE:
"On the Internet, no one knows you're a dog."

FAVORITE CELEBRITY:
(Okay enough, already—this is getting stupid)

CONCLUSION

NO, THERE WILL never be another Barney.

I find great joy in my new dog, Toby, and can honestly say I love him every bit as much as I did Barney. Toby is my friend, my companion. While there are striking similarities between the two, Toby has his own personality. Just like your kids, they are all different—loveable in their own way.

But I cannot ask Toby to fill those giant paw prints of his predecessor. The circumstances that led to the twelve years Barney spent on TV can never be duplicated. That is why Toby will not be on TV.

All of you have wonderful stories to tell about your own pets—stories that are as funny and as endearing as the ones I have shared in this book about Barney.

You may never write a book about your pet, but it is not necessary to fill pages with memories—only your heart.

Thanks for being one of Barney's fans. It has meant so much to both of us.

THANKS FOR THE MEMORIES

All of the Barney memorabilia that I collected over 13 years was displayed during the Deco' Down event in Fountain Square the weekend of June 4, 2004. An entire room was devoted to Barney's memory. Thanks to Judy and RJ Smith.

Was it a hit? Do you have to ask?

Coming soon from Dick Wolfsie and Gary Sampson, DVM:

Pet Peeves: Changing Eccentric Behavior in Dogs and Cats draws on Dr. Sampson's experiences from more than twenty years of counseling pet owners, coupled with Wolfsie's hilarious insights on those typical—and not so typical—days in the lives of pet owners. *Pet Peeves* will delight animal lovers with true dog and cat cases, while providing useful information on handling unusual situations with their own furry friends.

Read on for excerpts from *Pet Peeves*, forthcoming from Emmis Books in Spring 2005.

NOAH'S BARK

MRS. BAXTER'S DOG, Noah, was, to coin a phrase, a scaredy dog. Everything frightened him and sent him into a hissy-fit. The vacuum cleaner, the furnace, strangers at the front door, friends at the back door, the rattle of pans, the newspaper boy. Everything. You name it, he was scared of it. In fact, that's all you had to do was name it. "Noah, the mailman is here." He went berserk. And thunder—thunder turned Noah into a quivering little bundle of curly black hair. He didn't know where to turn. Actually, he did. He turned to Mrs. Baxter. And there was the problem.

Noah was small. He was a toy poodle. But size does not determine a dog's courage or sensitivity to sound or threat. Some of the biggest

Noah also had more than a touch of aggressiveness. One day Mrs. Baxter called the oven repairman who arrived at the front door and witnessed one of Noah's tantrums. He was amused to watch the little poodle erupt into a frenzy. Then he walked into the kitchen, bent way over, and stooped to look in the oven to fix the broken appliance. Noah took aim at the repairman's butt, latched on for dear life and would not let go. If you know anything about repairmen's butts, this was an easy target. That's when I got the phone call. I soon learned from my conversation with Mrs. Baxter that she and Noah spent every waking hour together and apparently the sleeping hours, as well. Noah even ate at the dinner table in his own high chair. I'm not advocating this, just reporting it.

Like any good parent, Mrs. Baxter was protective of her companion. When the front doorbell rang or the furnace kicked on, Mrs. Baxter picked up the yapping poodle, petted him, embraced him, coochie-cooed him to death.

When thunder struck, she lavished him with consoling affection. This was understandable, but a huge mistake. It wasn't long before Noah had it all figured out. "If I bark, quiver, shake and do my Don Knotts imitation, the old lady is going to pick me up and hug me." You had to get up pretty early in the morning to fool Noah. In fact, Noah probably liked storms. Forty days and nights of rain was fine with his namesake, after all.

To make matters worse, the dog had started nipping at people's heels at the front door, requiring Mrs. Baxter to pick Noah up to prevent him from biting. Instead of deterring this behavior, it emboldened Noah, who derived reinforcement from his owner. "Man, she loves this yapping, nipping, and protection thing," he must have thought. "Why else would she pick me up?"

Mrs. Baxter, who now feared a lawsuit from the oven repairman, had started putting Noah upstairs when the doorbell rang. NOT a good idea. Dogs who are isolated from interaction with strangers are perplexed by the new human scents they pick up in the house when released from their room. This only confuses the dog and makes the problem worse.

Here's the bottom line: Everything Mrs. Baxter did to prevent the inappropriate conduct was actually a motivation for Noah to continue his wayward actions. In fact, the more she tried to stop it, the worse it got. She was shaping his behavior. But not to the behavior she wanted.

As parents, we are cautioned about letting children enter our beds during a thunderstorm. We are encouraged instead to reason with them and to explain that the thunder cannot hurt them. Such reasoning and soothing doesn't work with dogs. It reinforces the behavior. Even dogs that are all ears, like beagles, cannot be convinced.

The solution was easy. Well, easy to prescribe, but tough for Mrs. Baxter. I instructed her to ignore the dog when he barked. Do not reward or punish him. Simply pay no attention, I told her. Then I told her again. I hoped she wasn't ignoring me. No, she was thinking about it.

"But what about the doorbell?" she asked. My suggestion was to tie the dog up about six feet from the door, preventing his ankle-nipping when the guest walked in. I also instructed Mrs. Baxter to give the "intruder" a treat to present to the dog, thus connecting the doorbell and the trespasser with positive reinforcement. Pavlov, eat your heart out.

Some people worry this approach will squelch the dog's natural instinct to be a protector. My experience convinces me that when real danger threatens, a dog instinctively knows from your demeanor—and possibly the odors that emanate from humans in time of peril—that this is for real. Any dog, even Noah, knows the difference between a burglar and a Boy Scout.

It took time, but eventually Noah learned not to overreact to every sound. Yes, everything was fine in the end. But try to tell that to the Maytag repairman.

HONEY DO

HONEY WAS NO ordinary cat. Actually, she was an ordinary cat. That's what makes this story so interesting. Honey's owner originally called because when she returned home from work each day she found cat feces all over the house. Not in any particular area, but everywhere. Feces under the dining room table, under the couch, in the corner of the room, under the coffee table. If feces had been eggs, this would have been a great Easter egg hunt.

"What about the litter box?" I asked. "Any waste in there?"

"Nothing. Absolutely nothing," came the reply.

Then I asked if the feces had any kitty litter on it. In other words, had the waste started in the box and then been taken out. The answer was complicated by the fact that the owner was using a clay kitty litter that did not cling to the dry feces.

I was hoping to discover if the cat was using the box or avoiding it altogether. My guess was that the cat was not using the box, a somewhat common problem that I had seen frequently.

To my surprise, upon close inspection, we discovered that all the waste did have litter on it. Which meant the cat was using the box. If the cat was using the box, and the waste was all over the house, the cat must have been batting the stuff around like a hockey player on uppers.

Cats, as a general rule, will not pick up feces with their teeth. I envisioned Honey doing her business, then swatting the "little gems" from the litter box with a perfect forehand, then playing kick the can with her waste material all through the house.

The implication of this brought a smirk to my face, which made me glad I did my diagnosis on the phone. Honey's owner would not have been amused.

But then I was stumped. Here's where a total pet history is important. As I continued to question Honey's owner, I learned she had not noticed the problem on weekends. This was a Monday through Friday occurrence, a little nugget of information that the client had not given much importance.

Often a behavioral diagnosis uncovers a slight change in a pet's routine leading to a change in the way the pet behaves. This was a perfect example.

Why did this not occur on the weekends? Because Honey was tended to, played with and loved on Saturdays and Sundays, but she was pretty much left to herself during the workweek. She was, quite literally, bored out of her feline skull. With no video games or a good book to occupy her time, she turned to field hockey. Her puck was a little unorthodox, but it served its purpose. It gave Honey something to do.

Cats love to sleep, often sixteen to twenty hours a day. But those waking hours require some stimulation. The difference between the attention Honey was paid on the weekends and the lack of activity during the week was too great. So Honey created her own intramural sport.

I was pretty sure I had made the right diagnosis, but successfully achieving a solution is the only way to prove a theory. The goal here (excuse the expression) was to control the boredom and keep the feces in the box.

Both were easily accomplished. We substituted a litter box with higher sides, making her slap shot nothing but a bank shot off the side wall. If Honey wanted to play with feces, she'd have to entertain herself in a cramped arena.

And, of course, I encouraged Honey's owner to provide some additional cat toys when she was absent during the workday and to be particularly loving and playful with Honey when she returned home each evening. That was the end of feline hockey. No more little pucks were found around the house and Honey never spent any time in the penalty box, just the litter box.

Also by Dick Wolfsie:

Life in a Nutshell: A Nutty Look at Life, Marriage, TV, and Dogs, is now available from Emmis Books. Read on for an excerpt from this collection of short essays—a wonderfully wacky take on daily life as only Dick Wolfsie can tell it.

SLEEPING AROUND

MY WIFE COMPLAINS about it. I brag about it. I think I'm one of those gifted men who can do it any time I want, day or night. I can do it for ten minutes or for the bulk of an afternoon. And I don't need some expensive pill. All I need is a bed. In fact, I don't even need a bed. That's how good I am.

Forgive me for shedding all pretense of modesty. I am the world's greatest napper.

Please, please—no applause. You might wake me up. Though I doubt it. When I was a high school teacher, I actually fell asleep in class while proctoring a statewide exam. The kids were very polite. "I hope we didn't disturb you yesterday, Mr. Wolfsie," said one of my students. "We tried to cheat as quietly as we could."

Here are some of my other conquests: I like to take a quick snooze while having dinner with friends, at stop signs, in movies, while waiting for my wife to put on makeup, while the dog is relieving himself, at fast-food drive-up windows, in check-out lines, in the dentist's office while waiting for root canal, in the dentist's chair during a root canal. "Wait a second," you say. "What about in front of the TV?" Please, please, don't confuse me with amateur nappets. It's that kind of self-indulgent behavior that gives professional nappers a bad name.

I do admit to having some regrets. Due to my heroic napping, I have missed a few events that, in retrospect, I probably should have stayed awake for. Here are the top three:

1. The wonder of natural childbirth
2. Paris
3. My fiftieth birthday (I wish they had screamed "surprise" louder.)

Now, I know what some of you women out there are saying: "You've never seen my husband, Harry. He's the worst." Of course, Harry is reading this and saying, "Hey, Wolfsie, you should see me. I'm the best."

Why do men and women place such different values on the siesta? Personally, I think women are afraid they're going to miss something. Like a sale, or a beautiful sunset, or the plot of a movie. Men don't care about stuff like this. If a woman should fall asleep during the day due to some freak circumstance, she would awaken with an apology to her family and an explanation of her behavior. "1 don't know what happened! That's just not like me. Why, I don't think I've done anything like that since we were married. I must be coming down with something." Men have a different attitude when awakening from a short slumber: "Man, that was a good nap. No, that was a great nap. You know, I'm getting better and better at this all the time."

Sometimes I worry about my son. As a toddler, he almost rivaled me, often falling asleep after a satisfying meal, sometimes actually sneaking in a nap before going to bed. I had great hopes for him. But lately I've begun to worry. No one wants to be disappointed in his own children, but I already see some disturbing signs: He reads an entire book without a yawn, gets through two video games without a stretch, and can actually sit through a movie without digging his nails into his thigh to wake himself up.

But he's still young and there is hope. The other day I passed his room after he had gone to bed. I could swear I heard the tiniest of snores. This is a good sign. Snoring is God's way of letting you brag about your napping, when you just don't have the energy to get out of bed and move to the couch.

BRAIN DRAIN

I CONSIDER MYSELF a pretty smart guy. Now, I know many of you who have seen me on TV, heard me on the radio, or read one of my news-paper columns think you have evidence to the contrary. The truth is I am very intelligent. Why, the people at MENSA claim that I would have clearly made it into their elite organization of high-IQ people if I hadn't gotten lost on the way to the exam.

You see, God works in mysterious ways. I clearly have some very special abilities. For example, if pushed, I could tell you fifty creative things to do with an old PEZ dispenser. Give me two completely unre-lated subjects, like cellular phones and French Lick, Indiana, and I can write a bawdy limerick about them in thirty seconds. If my wife asks me about a restaurant we went to ten years ago, I can tell her what we both had for dinner and what she was wearing.

I know what you're saying. These abilities don't seem to be very marketable. You're missing the point. God wanted me to have these rare talents, but it seemed unfair to endow one person with such genius with-out having him lack in other areas. As a result of the aforementioned blessings, the Lord has deemed that:

1. I will never have the slightest idea what a movie is about.

This drives my poor wife crazy. And I'm so paranoid about this that I start questioning her from the very moment we walk in the the-ater.

"Sweetheart, why did that man just jump off a cliff?"

"I don't know, Dick. Nor does anyone else. It's a preview."

Then the movie starts. I try to follow what's going on but I can't. "I'm sorry to bother you again, sweetheart, but why did that woman kill her husband?"

"Well let's see. During the hour we've been watching this, he has tried to strangle her, cheated on her, and kidnapped her father. Where have you been?"

"I guess my attention wandered. But I did think of the fifty-first thing to do with a PEZ dispenser."

2. I will have no sense of direction.

I cannot read a map. Give me a compass and a map, and I can make a very funny limerick using those two words, but I couldn't find my way out of a Plymouth minivan. On a map, north is up, south is down. I can't make this concept work for me in a three-dimensional world. When I take my family in the car on a vacation, I drive, my wife reads the map, and my twelve-year-old son explains the movie we saw the night before.

3. I will not be able to read instructions.

Nothing frustrates a person of my high intelligence more than this. There it is in black and white. In simple English. Also in Spanish, French, German, and Japanese. I'd be better off with the Japanese. Once, my wife came home and did pay me a compliment: "That is a nice Rubbermaid chaise lounge you assembled," she said proudly.

"Thank you," I beamed. "It was supposed to be a vertical storage cabinet."

And so, I recognize my limitations. I just wish my wife was a little easier on me. She won't go to the movies with me anymore because I ask so many stupid questions. So I took my son to see *Titanic*.

"Hey Dad. I don't care what Mom says. You're neat to go to the movies with. And entertaining, too."

"You think I'm entertaining?"

"Sure, like when you asked me why all those people were jumping overboard. That was really funny."

"Yeah, I guess I am pretty funny. Your mother just doesn't under-stand me."

COHABITATING

I DISCOVERED SOMETHING the other day about myself that is quite troubling. I guess my wife felt she had a responsibility to confront me with this. After all, I'm a mature adult; I have a family that needs me. I needed to face this:

She told me that I whistle.

I denied it. I find people who whistle to be annoying, rude, self-cen-tered, affected, and egocentric. But my wife was adamant. "You whistle," she said. "You've done it our entire marriage. I thought you knew. You do it when you're alone in your office or working in the garage. You've been whistling for twenty years. What really infuriates me is that you whistle while getting ready for work. Do you know how abnormal that is?"

"Why?"

"Why? Because 99 percent of all the men in the world hate their jobs. But you whistle on the way to work. Name one other person who does that."

"I can name seven. Dopey, Grumpy, Sleepy..."

"Very funny. I'm not counting your family."

Still unconvinced, I called my mother. "Mom, do I whistle?"

"Since you were a little boy. Yes, I used to call you 'my son the whistler,' which of course would make me—"

"Please, spare me, Mom. I'm depressed enough." How can a person have a bad habit like this for so long and never realize it? I wondered if I had any other habits that she found annoying after twenty years. I asked my wife. I shouldn't have.

"Do I have any other bad habits?"

"Not really," she said.

Which is somewhat equivalent to: "Let me make a list and I'll fax it to you in the morning."

"Come on. Name one more. I dare you."

"You're always bouncing your right leg. It started on our honeymoon. At first I thought it was some kind of mating ritual. It hasn't stopped for twenty years. You bounce your leg when you watch TV, when you have dinner, when you read the paper, at restaurants, at sporting events. Quite frankly, it drives me so crazy that sometimes I just want to go into the garage, get a sledge hammer, and crush your knee."

"Well, at least it's not a really annoying habit."

"Would you like to know what else you do? You make this little, moaning, guttural noise kind of in the bottom of your throat. I used to think it was kind of romantic, but you do it even when you clean out the kitty litter. If you're not whistling, that is!"

"Wow, I must be the world's most annoying person. Don't stop now."

"You stare into the refrigerator. You don't take anything out. You don't put anything in. You just stare. Then you close the door. And ten minutes later you come back and open the door again. And you just stare."

"Which part is the bad habit?"

"Look, Dick, you asked for help and all I get is an argument. Rather than wallowing in denial, it would be better for your mental health if you simply accepted your bad habits and worked to correct them. While your habits are annoying, and probably grounds for divorce in many states, I have come to love them as part of your overall makeup, you little leg-bouncing, whistling, moaner you. I even accept your slurping soup, drinking out of the milk carton, eating at the kitchen sink, even opening my mail. It's all just fine."

"Gee, if I'm that bad, why have you stayed married to me?"

"Heaven knows. You must be habit-forming."